The Existentialist's Guide to Death, the Universe and Nothingness

The **Existentialist's** Guide to Death, the Universe **and** Nothingness

Gary Cox

continuum

Continuum International Publishing Group

The Tower Building
11 York Road
London SE1 7NX

80 Maiden Lane
Suite 704
New York NY 10038

www.continuumbooks.com
www.garycoxphilosophy.com

British Library Cataloguing-in-Publication Data
A catalogue record for this book is available from the British Library.

ISBN: 978-1-4411-0783-1 (hardcover)

Library of Congress Cataloging-in-Publication Data
Cox, Gary, 1964-
The existentialist's guide to death, the universe, and nothingness / Gary Cox.
    p. cm.
Includes bibliographical references (p.   ) and index.
ISBN 978-1-4411-0783-1
1. Existentialism. 2. Conduct of life.
I. Title.
B819.C658 2011
142'.78–dc22   2011016334

Typeset by Amnet International, Dublin, Ireland
Printed and bound in India

Contents

Introduction

I've long been a fan of Douglas Adams' *The Hitchhiker's Guide to the Galaxy*, his fabulous guide to 'life, the universe and everything'. His unique blend of humour, science fiction and philosophy had a big influence on me as a youngster back in the 1980s and certainly helped inspire me to go ahead and study philosophy at university.

If I've got anywhere nearer to answering a central question that Adams poses – 'Why are people born? Why do they die? Why do they want to spend so much of the intervening time wearing digital watches?' (*The Hitchhiker's Guide to the Galaxy*, p. 119) – it is only to say that ultimately there is probably no reason for any of it. Adams' conclusion that forty-two is the 'answer' to the question, 'What is the meaning of life, the universe and everything?', aims to illustrate that there is really no satisfactory answer and that the problem lies in the question itself. Un-ask the question, as the Buddhists say.

Existentialists tend to argue that life only has the meaning each individual person chooses to give it. Thinking about the existentialists' response to Adams' question and how many of Adams' profound thoughts existentialists would identify with generally, started me thinking what an *existentialist's* guide to life, the universe and everything would be like. What ideas and themes would existentialists include in a guide aimed at the would-be existentialist wanting to hitchhike around the universe of existentialism?

Well, in such a guide there wouldn't be a lot of talk about space travel. Existentialists are very grounded creatures, not least in the sense of being preoccupied with down to earth human life, experience and interaction as lived and suffered in the urban environment. Still, what the existentialists say about the human condition would also apply to any aliens on other planets if, like us, those aliens were organic, embodied, conscious, intelligent, social and mortal.

The existentialists' view of human life is very much coloured by their view of mortality, their view that to be human is to be a *being-towards-death* engaged in an unavoidably finite life project. This is not morbidity on the part of existentialists, simply honesty and a no-nonsense approach to the so-called *fundamental existential truths of the human condition*. Their preoccupation with death as a fundamental truth would lead them, I think, to place 'death' as opposed to 'life' in the very title of their guide, just to remind people where existentialism is coming from philosophically and where we are all ultimately heading existentially.

Similarly, they would want to refer to 'nothingness' rather than 'everything' in the title of their guide because of the monumental role the phenomenon of nothingness plays in the existentialist world-view generally. As this guide explains, nothingness for existentialists is the basis of consciousness, and it is only when the negating power of consciousness arises that the universe gets carved up into the distinct phenomena that we experience. For existentialists, nothingness does not lie beyond the end of the universe. It is what each of us is – a nothingness in relation to being, endlessly striving to be at one with itself and the world. If you found this paragraph confusing yet strangely intriguing then this guide is definitely for you.

The Hitchhiker's Guide to the Galaxy famously warns its readers: 'Don't panic!' Existentialists certainly recognise the importance of not panicking when confronting life's many difficulties. Like Adams, they recommend facing up to reality with positive and decisive choices and actions. They might above all else, however, prefer to warn people: 'Don't despair!'

Even though life is ultimately absurd and pointless – anyone who doesn't see this is trying to live in a fairy tale – it is still possible to give life relative meaning and value by facing every challenge with courage and dignity and striving to achieve realistic goals. To set unrealistic goals is to try to live the fairy tale, it is to hanker after impossibilities like total happiness and complete fulfilment. The existentialists argue that if you want to be happy, or at least be happier, give up struggling for total happiness as that path inevitably leads to frustration and disappointment.

This guide explores a fascinating range of interrelated themes central to the philosophy of existentialism, from time, death and nothingness to love, hate and sexual desire. But a word of warning! This guide is full of tough, uncompromising existential truths about the human condition that some people will find physically, emotionally and philosophically disturbing. Existentialists are like everyone else – free, responsible, mortal, abandoned – the only difference is existentialists know it, don't try to deny it and strive to make the most of it. Welcome to the existentialists' hard-edged world-view. Can you handle it? Can you get real?

It is important to stress that this book is a *guide* to existentialism for people who may or may not be aspiring existentialists. It is not a rule book, a book of existentialist law saying existentialists must think this and do that – wear certain clothes, eat certain foods, perform certain rituals and mumble certain words. As the guide itself shows, existentialism is not about laying down the law like some fool religion designed for sheep. It is all about encouraging people to tune into their inalienable *freedom* and to think and act for themselves. Above all, it is about encouraging people to take personal *responsibility* for their choices rather than blaming the decisions they make and the actions they take on rules or the system or society or other people or the great wide indifferent universe generally.

You can dip into this guide or read it from cover to cover. I'm confident that either way you will get a huge amount out of it and will forevermore be the centre of attention at parties when the subject of existentialism crops up. If you don't go to the sort of parties where the subject of existentialism crops up then perhaps you are going to the wrong sort of parties. Wrong parties, right parties, it's all a matter of taste and personal choice, a matter of the value you yourself place on things.

You can certainly use this guide as a good, old-fashioned reference book, consulting it whenever you feel the need. Perhaps at difficult or special times and crucial crossroads in your life. At any time when you find yourself moved to ponder what it is existentialists tend to believe about freedom, anxiety, childhood, authenticity, indifference, sadomasochism, absurdity or God.

How you use this guide is of course your choice, as any existentialist worth his or her salt will tell you. Choose to use this guide for information and inspiration or choose to use it as a door wedge. Choose, if you must, to use it as a little rule book bible. However you use it, whatever you do, it's your doing, your existential choice, your responsibility, and no real business or concern of mine.

1 Existentialists and Existentialism

'What about you, madame?' he inquired. 'Are *you* an existentialist?' I can still recall my embarrassment at this question. (Simone de Beauvoir, *The Prime of Life*, p. 547)

An existentialist is a person whose work and ideas contribute to existentialism, or anyone who broadly subscribes to the theories and outlook of existentialism and attempts to live and die according to its principles. So, to understand what an existential*ist* is you need to understand what existential*ism* is. I'll explain what existentialism is shortly. Meanwhile, it is fair to say that to be a true existentialist a person has to know a fair amount about the philosophy and outlook of existentialism, more or less believe in existentialism rather than dismiss it as drivel and, above all, continually strive to live according to existentialism. She has to walk the walk of existentialism, not just talk the talk. She must continually strive to achieve what existentialist philosophers call *authenticity*.

Authenticity is the holy grail of existentialism, the great existentialist aspiration or ideal. Very simply, authenticity involves continually living according to the realisation that you are not a fixed entity like a rock or a table, defined entirely by circumstances, but a free being responsible for your choices. To live as though you are a fixed entity is what existentialist philosophers call *bad faith*. Bad faith is using freedom against itself by choosing not to choose, relinquishing responsibility and blaming other people and circumstances for the way you are and what you do. Existentialists despise bad faith. There are chapters in this book dedicated to both authenticity and bad faith.

Interestingly, it seems it is quite possible for a person to be authentic without ever having heard of existentialism. Otherwise, we would be claiming that authenticity can only be achieved as the result of a lot of bookworming. Some people seem to hit on being authentic through their direct experience of life or because they choose to be particularly brave, unselfish or original. We might call such people true existentialists, but really they are not existentialists at all, they are simply what swots who have studied existentialism describe as *authentic*.

They don't describe themselves as *authentic* because they don't think of themselves in that way. They just get on with absorbing themselves in whatever it is they do without self-consciousness, worries or regrets. It is not actually at all authentic for a person to think she is authentic. The person who declares 'I am authentic' thinks she *is* something, a fixed entity, an authentic-*thing*. A person who thinks like this or has this attitude is, in fact, in bad faith.

So, it is possible to be authentic without being an existentialist, but it is not possible to be a true existentialist without striving hard to be authentic. What matters is that the journey towards authenticity can begin with learning about existentialism. Many people have been inspired to pursue authenticity as a result of studying existentialism. Studying existentialism highlights the basic, inescapable, *existential truths* of the human condition, it exposes bad faith and emphasises the necessity of freedom and responsibility. Studying existentialism can, therefore, be a process of profound personal enlightenment that influences the very nature of a person's way of existing in the world.

So, what on earth is existentialism? Well, basically, existentialism is a broad intellectual movement of largely continental philosophers, psychologists, novelists, playwrights and other assorted egg-heads that developed in the nineteenth and twentieth centuries and remains influential today. The existentialist movement is defined by its shared concerns rather than by a set of common principles to which all existentialist thinkers subscribe, although there are principles common to many of them.

Existentialism is primarily concerned with providing a coherent description of the human condition that fully recognises and incorporates the fundamental or existential truths relating to that condition. Existentialism explores what it is for each of us to be in this bizarre and wicked world; what being alive in this world does and does not mean. It tells it like it is without going easy or bullshitting. The fundamental or existential truths of the human condition according to existentialism are as follows.

None of us are fixed entities like tables or stones, but indeterminate, ambiguous beings in constant process of becoming and change. We are all free and can't stop being free. We are all responsible for our actions and our lives are burdened with desire, guilt and anxiety, especially anxiety about what other people think of us. This leads us to suffer such bothersome emotions as guilt, shame and embarrassment. And, if all this isn't terrible enough, we are doomed to die from the moment we are born into a meaningless universe where there is no God, or at least a very elusive one. Amazingly, despite this tale of woe, existentialism is ultimately a positive and optimistic philosophy! But how can that be?

Well, because it outlines how a person can live a valuable life despite the fact that human existence is essentially meaningless and full of pain and misery. The general idea is that you can't create a genuinely honest and worthwhile life for yourself on the basis of a fantasy. You have to build your life on an understanding and acceptance of how things really are, otherwise you will always be fooling and deluding yourself as you yearn to live happily ever after. Only the person wise enough to become disenchanted with chasing the illusion of *total* satisfaction can hope to achieve *relative* satisfaction.

In a philosophical essay he wrote called *The Myth of Sisyphus*, the existentialist philosopher, Albert Camus, compares human existence to the plight of the mythical figure Sisyphus who is condemned forever to push a large rock to the top of a hill only to watch it roll down again. Camus asks if life is worth living given that it is as absurd and ultimately futile as the plight of Sisyphus. 'There is but one truly serious philosophical problem and that is suicide. Judging whether life is or is not worth living amounts to answering the fundamental question of philosophy' (*The Myth of Sisyphus*, p. 11).

In choosing to live, in refusing the ever present possibility of suicide, a person confers value and significance on a life that has no value or significance in itself. In choosing to live her life rather than end it a person takes on responsibility for her life. Camus' seemingly pessimistic account of the existential truths of the human condition yields an optimistic conclusion: although life's struggle has no ultimate purpose and always the same end result, a person can still create a sense of purpose through the struggle itself and through the way she plays life's game. If you think this is not a very optimistic conclusion then I challenge you to come up with a more optimistic conclusion that isn't based on false assumptions about the way life really is, a conclusion that isn't just a deluded wish list when you look at it honestly.

It was the eccentric Christian philosopher Søren Kierkegaard and the atheistic, romantic philosophers, Arthur Schopenhauer and Friedrich Nietzsche, who, in their different ways, set the agenda for what later became known as existentialism. All three of them were concerned with identifying and exploring the perennial truths of the human condition.

The concerns of Kierkegaard, Schopenhauer and Nietzsche were taken up during the first half of the twentieth century by Karl Jaspers in his *existence philosophy*, and by Martin Heidegger, Jean-Paul Sartre, Simone de Beauvoir, Maurice Merleau-Ponty and Albert Camus. The last four in this list all knew each other and hung out together in Parisian cafés in the 1930s and '40s, chain-smoking and discussing the enormous books they were working on.

The writings of Heidegger, Sartre and the rest established existentialism as a distinct branch of philosophy. The ideas of these philosophers converge to form a largely coherent system of thought. At the heart of their system is the maxim 'existence precedes essence'. This maxim is generally attributed to Sartre who certainly uses it in his 1946 book, *Existentialism and Humanism*. It sums up a view fundamentally opposed to idealism that there are no ideal, otherworldly, God-given, abstract, metaphysical essences giving reality or meaning to particular things. There are particular things, like tables and stones, and there is nothing beyond the series of particular things other than consciousness, which is nothing more than consciousness *of* particular things.

Consciousness or the mind, the existentialists argue, is a *nothingness*. It is not a thing in its own right but a *relation*. Like a reflection in a mirror it is entirely comprised of what it reflects. Because consciousness is nothing in itself, each person is nothing in herself. As said, nobody is a fixed entity. Not being fixed entities, people must continually strive to *be* something; to create themselves through the choices they make and the actions they take.

With specific regard to people, 'existence precedes essence' refers to the view that each person exists first, without meaning or purpose, and strives thereafter to give herself meaning and purpose. A person's essence is to have no essence other than the 'essence' she must continually invent for herself. As Simone de Beauvoir famously argued throughout her many writings, 'Man's nature is to have no nature'.

There is a religious branch of existentialism founded by Kierkegaard which is explored in the penultimate chapter, but mainstream existentialism is anti-idealist, anti-metaphysical and atheistic. It sees mankind as occupying an indifferent universe that is meaningless to the point of absurdity. Any meaning that is to be found in this world must be established by each person from within the sphere of her own individual existence. A person who supposes that her meaning comes ready-made or that there is an ultimate purpose to human existence established externally by a deity or deities is shying away from reality and living a lie.

Existentialism is a largely coherent theory of the human condition rooted in the best traditions of western philosophy. It is really all based on a theory of the nature of human consciousness, the roots of which can be traced back to the brilliant German philosopher, Immanuel Kant, and his equally brilliant successor, George W. F. Hegel. Existentialism is in fact only a branch or a development of a philosophical theory called *phenomenology* which can certainly be traced back to Hegel and, to some extent, Kant as well, although Kant was hugely influenced by the Scottish empiricist philosopher, David Hume. And so it goes, back down the foggy ruins of time, back to the first prehistoric cave person with a half-decent meal inside her who, finding she was not about to be devoured by wolves, looked up at the stars or down into a chasm and asked herself, what is the meaning of death, the universe and nothingness?

2   The Universe

We are just an advanced breed of monkeys on a minor planet of a very average star. But we can understand the Universe. That makes us something very special.
(Stephen Hawking, *Der Spiegel,* 17 October 1988)

Existentialists don't really have much to say about the universe as such, the stars and galaxies of the astronomers or the vastness of outer space. If they evoke the scientific notion of the universe at all, it is to reinforce their nihilistic claims about how lost and abandoned humanity is in the so-called grand scheme of things (what scheme?) and how ultimately pointless and absurd our futile, ant-swarm existence is on this speck of space debris we call Earth.

Neither are existentialists particularly concerned about whether or not there is intelligent life on other planets. Yes, it would be interesting even to an existentialist to discover aliens exist – more 'other people' to feel threatened by and anxious about – but it would not fundamentally change anything. The aliens would be equally lost and abandoned in a meaningless universe, equally devoid of ultimate purpose, equally condemned to be free, equally confused and perplexed by the series of cosmic accidents that bought them into existence on their own speck of space debris.

The existentialists' lack of interest in the universe of the astronomers and astrophysicists is partly a result of their lack of faith in science. Existentialists are not anti-science or anti-scientific progress, they leave that to the Amish and the Luddites. They recognise that in many respects science has improved the way a lot of things work and are not averse to enjoying the benefits of science and technology. Sartre and de Beauvoir loved to travel by plane, train and automobile. But they also recognise in their very post-modern way that science cannot alter or abolish the fundamental existential truths of the human condition.

Science will never eliminate pain and suffering, for example. Okay, it has given us some pretty nifty antibiotics and painkillers, but it has also given us oil spills, global warming and nuclear holocaust, and doubtless it has further horrors up its nylon sleeve. Science has helped many people to live longer, to prolong their futile existence, but it will never allow us to live forever, and even if it could, would anyone still want to live forever after a few centuries of taking out the trash? A robot can take out the trash, I hear you cry. But why live if our servants can live for us? Science can attempt to alleviate our existential fears and anxieties but only by counselling us into phoney over-optimism or by prescribing courses of happy pills that transform us into two-dimensional Prozac-driven zombies.

However advanced technology becomes, however many useful little apps we have on our idiotic i-phones, -pads and -pods, it will never enable us to overcome our vulnerability, anxiety or mortality; our confusion about who we are and what we want. We will still be confronted each day with hard existential choices about what to do and who to be, about what to strive for and what to value. Science and technology can do nothing to change the existential truth that essentially humans can never be totally and permanently fulfilled and will always find something lacking. However many goodies the modern world offers, boredom and dissatisfaction will always rear their ugly heads.

The existentialist universe is a much more down to earth, non-scientific affair than that of the astronomer or cosmologist. It is the everyday world of the individual person who, confronted by obstacles, challenges and other people, must continually make choices about how she will or will not deal with these difficulties. In the classic writings of the existentialist philosophers, this universe, this succession of situations demanding a response, consists almost entirely of a series of dingy urban rooms occupied by angst ridden adults obsessing over their relationships; Parisian apartments and sleazy basement nightclubs thick with tobacco smoke where every sad customer is a drugged or drunken washout. Criticising existentialism, the philosopher Mary Midgley writes:

> The impression of *desertion* or *abandonment* which existentialists have is due, I am sure, not to the removal of God, but to this contemptuous dismissal of almost the whole biosphere – plants, animals, and children. Life shrinks to a few urban rooms; no wonder it becomes absurd. (*Beast and Man*, pp. 18–19)

Certainly there is little or nothing of the natural world in classic existentialism – mountains, lakes, waterfalls, roaring oceans – and definitely no celebration of it. At most there are municipal parks where the trees are not pretty or shady but encapsulate the nauseating absurdity of brute, naked, superfluous existence. As Sartre writes in his cult existentialist novel, *Nausea*:

> I was in the municipal park just now. The root of the chestnut tree plunged into the ground just underneath my bench. I no longer remembered that it was a root. Words had disappeared, and with them the meaning of things, the method of using them, the feeble landmarks which men have traced on their surface. I was sitting, slightly bent, my head bowed, alone in front of that black knotty mass, which was utterly crude and frightening to me. (*Nausea*, p. 182)

Existentialists, perhaps, would have more inspiring notions of the physical universe if they got out of town more and met with the majesty of nature on a grand scale. But as they would argue, to speak of the majesty of nature is a value judgement, and probably a petty-bourgeois value judgement at that.

I must add, for what it is worth, that de Beauvoir and Sartre were fond of cycling and world travel, activities likely to put a person in touch with the natural world, although it depends where a person goes of course. For a lot of people, 'world travel' means flying to Disneyland, Florida to meet the real Mickey Mouse – something which, for many an existentialist, undoubtedly encapsulates the nauseating absurdity of brute, naked, superfluous existence.

Existentialists may not be interested in cosmology but they are interested in ontology – philosophical enquiry into the fundamental nature of existence or reality. They do not follow the physicists in postulating ever more fundamental particles and packets of energy, dark matter, silly string, whatever. For the existentialists, what there is, ontologically speaking, what there is fundamentally, is *being*, plain and simple. Certainly, in *Being and Nothingness*, a huge volume that many people refer to as the bible of existentialism, Sartre is very taken with the notion of *being-in-itself*. What there is fundamentally, according to Sartre, is not the universe of diverse and complex phenomena that we perceive all around us, but being-in-itself.

Also referred to as undifferentiated being, being-in-itself is the basis or starting point of the ontology of Sartre and his followers. Every phenomenon they go on to describe ultimately depends on being-in-itself for its existence. Consciousness, for example, or what they generally refer to as nothingness or non-being or being-*for*-itself, exists only as the negation or denial of being-in-itself. As such, consciousness is entirely dependent on being-in-itself because it is nothing but being-in-itself *denied*. Nothingness and consciousness are explored in detail in the next two chapters.

All that can really be said about being-in-itself is that it *is*. It is its own foundation. That is, it is founded upon itself and therefore not dependent upon anything else. It is that which exists fundamentally, *in itself*, in its own right, rather than being that which does not exist in itself and is dependent upon something else for its existence. It is self-sufficient, uncreated and unchanging.

It is tempting to suppose that being-in-itself has always been and will always be, and even Sartre refers to eternity in describing it.

Being-in-itself, however, is eternal only in the sense of being timeless. There is no before or after, past or future, for being-in-itself. Time or temporality exists only for a being that is perpetually not what it was and not yet what it will be, namely consciousness. For much more on this see the chapter on time that follows the chapter on consciousness and lack.

It is also tempting to suppose that the existence of being-in-itself is necessary. However, to describe being-in-itself as a necessity is to characterise it as that which cannot not be, when it has no characteristics whatsoever other than *being*. Being-in-itself exists utterly, yet its existence is not necessary. It *is*, yet it need not be. It exists without reason or justification. This is the all important contingency, superfluity or even absurdity of being-in-itself that existentialists are so obsessed with, the absurdity that Sartre describes so powerfully in his aforementioned novel, *Nausea*. Contingency and absurdity are the focus of Chapter 18.

It is also tempting to suppose that because being-in-itself exists it must be the realisation of a possibility, that it must be derived from the possible. Possibility, however, exists only from the point of view of consciousness which cannot pre-exist being-in-itself, so being-in-itself cannot be identified or characterised as the realisation of what is possible. Being-in-itself is not derived from the possible and neither does it have possibilities.

For its part, consciousness has a future in which to realise and actualise its possibilities, but being-in-itself, as said, has no future, or past, and therefore possibility is not a quality that can be discovered in it or applied to it.

That being-in-itself has no characteristics leads some existentialists to describe it as *undifferentiated being*, a way of stressing that it is devoid of contrasts, divisions and differences. No part of it is any different from any other part of it, which is to say, it does not have parts. It is not a necessity, it has no possibilities, it is not temporal or even spatial. It should not even be thought of as an infinite block of physical stuff, although existentialists do sometimes refer to physical objects as beings in themselves in contrast to persons who are beings for themselves ceaselessly striving to be beings in themselves.

If being-in-itself were spatial it would be differentiated in the sense of having different regions, here and there and so on, but being-in-itself has no regions or parts just as it has no past or future. Unlike its negation – consciousness or being-for-itself – being-in-itself is never *other* than itself. It is what it is, whereas consciousness is perpetually and paradoxically what it is not and not what it is.

The philosopher Hegel, not an existentialist but a big early influence on existentialist thinking, argues that being is so undifferentiated and featureless that it is in fact indistinguishable from non-being or nothingness! For Hegel, there is neither being nor non-being but only *becoming*. Sartre, for one, disagrees with Hegel, insisting that being-in-itself *is* while non-being or nothingness *is not*. For Sartre, being-in-itself is logically primary. All else – i.e. non-being – is logically subsequent to being, dependent upon it and derived from it.

As said, being-in-itself has a negation in the form of consciousness. It is tempting to suppose that being-in-itself gave rise to its negation, as though giving rise to its negation was a *project* on the part of being-in-itself. Being-in-itself, however, because it is what it is and cannot be other than what it is, cannot have projects or conceive of possibilities. So, the question is, how did consciousness arise as the negation of being-in-itself?

Sartre insists, though not all scholars agree with him, that it is impossible to answer this question and that any attempt to account for what he describes as the *upsurge* of consciousness from being-in-itself produces only theories that can never be shown to be true or false. For Sartre, the upsurge of consciousness must be accepted as a fundamental, axiomatic truth, just as the being of being-in-itself must be accepted as a fundamental, axiomatic truth. A truth beyond which it is impossible to go.

As existentialist ontology is abstract stuff and can be rather mind-bending, here is a summary of the existentialist position regarding being-in-itself. being-in-itself *is*. It is not created, changing, temporal, necessary, physical or spatial. It has no characteristics other than being, and it is not differentiated in any way. It has a negation that Sartre describes as being-for-itself or consciousness, a negation that is entirely dependent upon being-in-itself for its borrowed being. The emergence or upsurge of this negation from being-in-itself is, for Sartre, an unfathomable mystery. All those phenomena that comprise the human world, many of which are explored in this book – change, time, possibility, spatiality, lack, freedom, love, death and so on – arise through the *relationship* between consciousness and being-in-itself and exist only from the perspective of consciousness.

So, the existentialist universe does not consist of atoms, electrons, quarks or whatever fundamental entities physicists are promoting this year. All that diversity and complexity comes later, from the point of view of the observer, from the point of view of consciousness. For existentialists, mankind is the measure of all things and apart from consciousness, human and animal, there is only undifferentiated being-in-itself. 'Uncreated, without reason for being, without any connection with another being, being-in-itself is *de trop* for eternity' (*Being and Nothingness*, p. 22). Existentialists have quite a mystical view of the universe for such down to earth philosophers.

3   Nothingness

God made everything out of nothing. But the nothingness shows through.
(Paul Valéry, *Mauvaises Pensées et Autres* [*Bad Thoughts and Others*], p. 503)

Warning! This chapter is mind-bendingly abstract but essential reading if you want to learn about the logical or ontological bones that form the supporting skeleton of existentialism. If you like to get beneath the skin of things as all good philosophers do, it should not bother you that this load of old bones is as dry as a Saharan drought. I am confident that if you persist with it, and maybe re-read the more difficult bits, it will eventually make sense. After all, I'm no genius and I understand it.

To truly understand existentialism it is vital to·understand the all important role existentialists ascribe to nothingness or non-being. It is not really possible to explain the existentialist view of nothingness without knitting together convoluted strings of negations that at first sight appear absurd – talk of x not being what it is and being what it is not and stuff like that. With a bit of focus, however, these strings of negations can be grasped and traced back to a most subtle and profound view of reality.

Basically, what has to be kept in mind is that not everything in reality is a thing. The universe, at least as we encounter it, is comprised of a lot of entities that do not exist in their own right but only in *relation* to things that do exist. We constantly encounter the world and make sense of it in terms of what is not there, in terms of what is lacking or absent, in terms of various nothingnesses or negativities.

You so wanted to see him, to be with him, but he was *not* at the party as you expected. His absence from the party is not a ghostly fog that pervades the party but a nothingness that you place there on the grounds of your expectation of his presence and your desire for it. This absence, this nothingness, although it is nothing, characterises the whole party for you. I offer this example because it is probably one you are familiar with from your own life experience. Hopefully, it serves to remind you that you already have a sense of the crucial role nothingness plays in your life, in all our lives. Half moon, half empty glass, unbaked cake, yesterday is just a memory, tomorrow never comes, nothing was done, nobody saw.

> 'Who did you pass on the road?' the King went on, holding out his hand to the Messenger for some more hay.
>
> 'Nobody,' said the Messenger.
>
> 'Quite right,' said the King: 'this young lady saw him too. So of course Nobody walks slower than you.'
>
> 'I do my best,' the Messenger said in a sulky tone. 'I'm sure nobody walks much faster than I do!'
>
> (Lewis Carroll, *Through the Looking Glass*, pp. 114–115)

Anyway, being *is* and nothingness *is not*. What could be simpler than that? But nothingness cannot simply be its own nothingness otherwise it would be absolutely nothing at all and there would only be being-in-itself as described in the previous chapter. For nothingness to have some kind of existence, albeit a negative existence, for it to play the important role it undoubtedly plays in shaping reality, nothingness cannot be a nothingness in itself, simply nothing. It must actively be the nothingness, the denial, the negation of being-in-itself. Nothingness, the existentialists say, is being *denied*. That is, nothingness or non-being requires being in order to be the denial or negation of it.

To put it slightly more formally, which may well help your understanding, existentialist philosophers say, non-being – as the negation of being – is ontologically dependent upon being. Being, of course, is not ontologically dependent upon non-being because, as we noted above, being is and nothingness is not. Being has no need of nothingness in order to exist. It has logical precedence over nothingness. But nothingness needs being even more than gin needs tonic because nothingness is nothing more than the nothingness, the denial, the negation, of being.

Let's try and nail all this down. Take a deep breath and be prepared to re-read. Being-in-itself, unlike nothingness, is what it is and not what it is not. Nevertheless, what it is not (nothingness) *is*. Not in the sense of being it – that would make nothingness indistinguishable from being-in-itself – but in the sense of *having to be* it. Unlike being-in-itself, which simply *is* without having to do anything to achieve its being, nothingness has to achieve, *for itself*, its being as the non-being of being-in-itself by perpetually negating being-in-itself. It has to be what it is *for itself* as the active negation of being-in-itself. Hence, some existentialists, Sartre in particular, call non-being *being-for-itself* or *the for-itself*.

The for-itself is the negation of being. It is being first posited then denied. It is not the non-being of itself, it is the non-being of being. In not being the non-being of itself, the for-itself has to perpetually strive to be the non-being of itself without ever being able to become non-being-in-itself, or what Sartre and company call *being-for-itself-in-itself*.

Being-for-itself-in-itself is a perpetually desired but absolutely unrealisable state of being in which the negation of being becomes a self-sufficient negation-in-itself. It is the impossible fusion of being-for-itself and being-in-itself. In other words, it is an impossible state of being in which the nothingness that is the essence of being-for-itself exists with the full positivity of being-in-itself.

Interestingly, it is widely held that God exists in this way. God is essentially a being-for-itself, a conscious, knowing being, yet his consciousness is held to exist fundamentally rather than as a relation to being or a negation of it. 'I am that I am' said God, impersonating a burning bush (Exodus 3:14). In short, God's existence and essence are assumed to be one and the same. God is the ultimate for-itself-in-itself. This is why some existentialists argue that the fundamental, unrealisable project of being-for-itself – the fundamental, unrealisable project of human conscious-ness – is to be God! Deep down we are all megalomaniacs.

If being-for-itself achieved identity with itself it would become being-in-itself; it would collapse back into being. Therefore, the for-itself has both to be the perpetual project of negating being in order to realise itself as the negation of being, and the perpetual project of negating itself in order to refuse a coincidence with itself that would be its own annihilation. The for-itself cannot coincide with itself and, indeed, it exists by virtue of continually not coinciding with itself and, so to speak, avoiding itself. In order not to collapse back into being – or, to be more precise, in order not to collapse into a pure non-being that left only being – the for-itself must be both an affirmation denied and a denial affirmed.

The affirmation that is denied is being-in-itself. The denial that is affirmed is the for-itself's denial of itself as denial-in-itself; that is, the denial of itself as for-itself-in-itself. Unable to be a being fixed and determinate in itself, either as being or as non-being, the for-itself has to be a perpetually ambiguous, indeterminate and paradoxical being. It has to be a perpetual *double negation*.

In describing the paradoxical nature of the for-itself Sartre says repeatedly in *Being and Nothingness* that the for-itself is *a being which is not what it is and which is what it is not*. In one place Sartre says, 'At present it is not what it is (past) and it is what it is not (future)' (*Being and Nothingness*, p. 146), revealing that the ambiguous, paradoxical nature of the for-itself is best understood in terms of time or temporality. Time is the focus of Chapter 5.

It has been more than hinted at several times already that nothingness, non-being, negation, being-for-itself is the essence of consciousness. Consciousness is, according to the existentialists, a nothingness in relation to being. Hopefully, the rather dry explanation of the being-nothingness relationship thrashed out in this chapter will help justify the various bold claims made in the following chapter on the existentialist view of consciousness, and generally render that chapter and all those that follow it far more accessible, coherent and credible than they might otherwise be. Tough and even tedious though it is to do, it is always necessary when philosophising to lay firm logical foundations that prevent the structure on top from collapsing into the mire.

Besides, I had to include this chapter to justify the catchy title of this book. Or rather, the title of this book, an inverted paraphrase of the famous Douglas Adams expression, 'Life, the universe and everything', obliged me to include this chapter.

4 Consciousness and Lack

The living substance is that being which is truly subject ... As subject it is pure and simple negativity. (George Wilhelm Friedrich Hegel, *The Phenomenology of Mind*, p. 16)

Hopefully the previous chapter, if you've read it, has allowed you to get a reasonable grasp on the initially weird sounding claim that consciousness, the consciousness of each human being, is essentially a nothingness, negativity or non-being in relation to the world.

Consciousness does not exist as a thing, it is not any kind of object. It is not a mental substance, as the philosopher Descartes supposed, existing in its own right and then entertaining thoughts. In fact, it is nothing in itself. It exists only in relation to what it is consciousness *of*. If it were not conscious of anything it would not exist. Existentialists sum this view up with the maxim: consciousness is consciousness of __. As Sartre writes in *Being and Nothingness*, 'To say that consciousness is consciousness of something means that for consciousness there is no being outside of that precise obligation to be a revealing intuition of something' (*Being and Nothingness*, p. 17).

The theory that consciousness exists only in so far as it intends something or is about something is known, not surprisingly, as the theory of *intentionality* or *aboutness*. This theory, one of the philosophical cornerstones of existentialism, was first put forward by the German philosopher and psychologist, Franz Brentano, who introduced the idea in his book, *Psychology from an Empirical Standpoint*. Brentano writes:

> Every mental phenomenon includes something as object within itself, although they do not all do so in the same way. In presentation something is presented, in judgement something is affirmed or denied, in love loved, in hate hated, in desire desired and so on. This intentional inexistence is characteristic exclusively of mental phenomena. No physical phenomena exhibit anything like it. We can, therefore, define mental phenomena by saying that they are those phenomena which contain an object intentionally within themselves. (*Psychology from an Empirical Standpoint*, pp. 88–89)

The theory of intentionality implies that because consciousness is always of or about something and nothing beyond that, any attempt by philosophers to investigate consciousness and say what it is must always lead immediately to an investigation and a certain kind of description of whatever consciousness is of or about. The philosophy of Brentano, Husserl, Sartre and others, formally known as *phenomenology*, seeks to understand consciousness by investigating and describing the way in which different *phenomena*, different *intentional objects*, appear to consciousness. An intentional object is whatever consciousness is *about*, be it seen, imagined, believed or felt.

Jealousy, for example, is an intentional object, a collection of appearances to consciousness. Nick's jealousy of David, for example, does not exist as such. It is an intentional object (in this case an intentional psychic object) comprised of Nick's resentment when he sees David, his unacknowledged sense of inferiority when he thinks of David, the negative things he says about David, his wish or intention to get the better of David and so on. These appearances are not manifestations of an underlying jealousy, they are the jealousy. There is no jealousy in itself beyond the various appearances that we collectively describe as Nick's jealousy of David.

A physical object is also an intentional object, a collection of appearances to consciousness. Just as jealousy is comprised of various appearances, so a physical object is comprised of various appearances too. We

like to think that the physical object itself exists beneath the appearances, but really a physical object is nothing more than a collection of
appearances that emerge, alter and disappear according to distance,
point of view, light and so on.

Close up a cup appears large. If the cup is turned about different
sides appear successively. Its shape appears differently as its orientation
changes and its colour appears to alter with the light. The cup makes a
sound as it is placed back on its saucer. Far away the cup appears small.
When reduced to its appearances in this way the physical object does
not appear, but rather a succession of aspects. Really, there are no
physical objects in themselves. There is nothing beyond the various
shifting appearances that we collectively describe as this or that physical object other than undifferentiated being-in-itself.

Many existentialists argue for a featureless, undifferentiated being-
in-itself that is differentiated into distinct phenomena by consciousness. Consciousness, they argue, is a negation that places particular
negations or negativities into being that, so to speak, slice being up
into particular phenomena. Basic distinctions, divisions and differences
arise that always involve nothingness or negation – here is *not* there,
this is *not* that and so on. Earlier, we said that being-in-itself is not
temporal or spatial, which is to say, it is not in time and space. Amazingly, time and space only exist from the point of view of consciousness. Or, to put it another way, there is no time and space apart from
consciousness. It is consciousness that imposes time and space on
undifferentiated being in order to differentiate it.

In his great work, *The Critique of Pure Reason*, one of the most influential works of philosophy ever written, Immanuel Kant describes time
and space as pure *a priori* forms of intuition, arguing that we do not
actually *experience* time and space, but rather that we experience *in
terms of* time and space. *A priori* means *prior to experience*. Kant's pure
intuitions are *a priori* because they are prior to experience. We do not
experience them. Rather, they are the basic organisational framework
of each person's experience of the world. Time and space are the *way*

consciousness organises the world. Believe it or not, just as you have never experienced 'to the left of' in itself, only particular things being to the left of other things, you have never experienced time in itself or space in itself, only a world structured and organised spatio-temporally.

Sartre, who is very much a post-Kantian in a lot of his thinking, argues that being-for-itself or consciousness is grounded upon being-in-itself, while differentiated being, the richly varied world of phenomena we all inhabit, is grounded upon consciousness, or at least, upon the negations that consciousness places into being. Sartre argues that phenomena (what appears) are not grounded upon being but upon particular *privations* or *lacks* of being. Particular privations of being occur when, for example, being is questioned.

The relationship of consciousness to the world is primarily characterised by a questioning attitude. This attitude is not just the capacity to judge that something is lacking but the constant expectation of a discovery of non-being. If I look to see if my pie is cooked, for example, it is because I consider it possible that it is *not* cooked. Even supposing there are pies apart from consciousness of them, a pie can only be 'not cooked' for a consciousness that experiences the pie in the mode of not yet being what it will be in future. The pie does not lack being cooked for itself, it lacks being cooked for a consciousness that has desires and expectations with regard to pies.

Consciousness constantly introduces non-being, negation, negativities, lack, absence into the world in order to make sense of it and to act purposefully within it. In abstract, technical terms we might say phenomena are grounded not upon being but upon non-being. They arise for being-for-itself when being-for-itself places particular negativities into undifferentiated being thus giving rise to differentiated being.

In slightly more down to earth terms we might say a situation is always understood not in terms of what it is but in terms of what it lacks for the consciousness encountering it. In itself a situation is a fullness of being, it lacks nothing, but in itself it is precisely not a situation because to be a situation it must be a situation for someone, the situation of someone. The lacks that make it a situation, that give it future possibilities and so on, are given to it by the consciousness, the person, for whom it is a situation.

Existentialists insist that a person interprets every situation according to her desires, hopes, expectations and intentions. Every situation a person encounters is understood as presently lacking something desired, expected, intended or anticipated. As said, the situation in itself does not lack anything; it lacks something for the person whose situation it is. Consciousness is always predisposed to find something lacking. Indeed, lack is intrinsic to the very meaning of every situation for any particular consciousness.

Every situation is a situation for consciousness. Consciousness, as that which exists by negating the situation, must be situated in order to be. Consciousness, for which the situation is a situation, is not a part of the situation but rather the negation of the situation. It transcends the situation in order to realise the situation. Every situation is understood not in terms of what it is but in terms of what it lacks, and what every situation lacks is precisely consciousness or being-for-itself. Consciousness is those particular lacks that determine the situation as a situation.

You go into a pub and order a pint of beer. To your annoyance the slack barman pours you less than a pint. What is called in the trade, a short measure. Now, in itself a short measure is neither complete nor incomplete, it is simply what it is. In order to understand it as the partial appearance of a pint it must be judged in terms of the pint of beer that is presently lacking. The meaning of the short measured beer is founded upon the non-being of the full pint of beer which the short measured beer lacks. The short measured beer does not lack the full pint of beer for itself. The short measured beer lacks the full pint of beer for an expectant consciousness that is the surpassing of the existence of the short measure towards the non-existence of the full pint. It is the non-being of the full pint that gives the short measure its meaning for consciousness as a short measure. For consciousness, the short measure exists in the mode of being the non-being of the full measure. As that which is given, the short measure is what it is. As a meaningful phenomenon, the short measure is understood as what it is by virtue of what it lacks.

In so far as consciousness is those particular lacks that determine the situation, it is itself a lack. It is not a being in its own right but the negation of being. It is a nothingness, but not a passive nothingness. If it was simply and passively its own nothingness it would instantly vanish. It would be nothing at all. So it must endlessly strive to overcome its nothingness by trying to become a being in its own right. But if it became a being in its own right it would cease to exist as the negation of being and would merge into the world rather than be consciousness of the world. It is always caught, and must always be caught if it is to have any reality at all, between total nothingness and total being. In order to be, it must always be ambiguous and paradoxical. It must incessantly be what it is not and not be what it is.

Consciousness constantly strives to become a being that is identical with itself yet still conscious. This is impossible because consciousness must always be constituted as a negation. The first rule of all consciousness is 'I am *not* this'. That is to say, in order to be consciousness of a thing I must not be that thing or any kind of thing. Only a nothingness can 'stand back' from the world in order to be aware of the world.

As was said in the previous chapter, the impossible state of being that consciousness strives to achieve is what Sartre and others call being-for-itself-in-itself. Consciousness yearns to be fulfilled and at one with itself, to be a being-in-itself rather than a lack, yet somehow a being-in-itself that is still conscious. All human desire aims at this god-like state of self-identity and self-fulfilment. Alas, as any existentialist will tell you, although it is possible to satisfy a particular desire, to overcome a particular lack, it is not possible to satisfy desire as such, to overcome lack as such.

The fact that being-for-itself is always constituted as a lack led Sartre to conclude that 'Man is a useless passion' (*Being and Nothingness*,

p. 636). 'If I could get that guy,' sighs the lover, 'I would never want anything again,' fooling herself that by getting the guy she would achieve the impossible and become a permanently fulfilled lack. Establishing a relationship with the guy might briefly enchant her into thinking she has achieved complete and lasting fulfilment, but she will soon come to have various desires with regard to their relationship: the desire for him to treat her in a certain way, to remain faithful, to get on with her friends. The desire for marriage and children or the unforeseen, gradually emerging desire for an end to their relationship.

Constituted as the lack that it has to be, being-for-itself cannot be completely fulfilled. As the negation of being it must surpass any particular obtained object of desire towards a further un-obtained object of desire. When we are completely satisfied with a particular thing we soon refocus our attention on something else we are not satisfied with. When I am satisfied with this paragraph I will move on to the next. Satisfied or not with today's writing, other desires will draw me away from my desk. The desire to clear my head, the desire to eat, to exercise, to mow the lawn. Ever onward, seeking an unobtainable fulfilment somewhere in the future until there is no more future to come. It is sometimes said that sleep offers a temporary escape from the incessant parade of desires, but surely our dreams heave with longing and the imagined satisfaction of some of our deepest yearnings.

Closely linked to the phenomenon of existential lack is the phenomenon of existential absence. Your best friend, Angela, is absent from Starbucks where you arranged to meet her. The network is down so unusually you can't phone her to find out where she is. As you look high and low for her, everything in Starbucks becomes background with her absence as a kind of foreground. She is perpetually about to appear against this background but doesn't. Angela, as the person you expect to find, is existentially absent from Starbucks.

This *existential absence* is distinct from an abstract and purely *formal absence* that is merely thought. Michael Jackson is not in Starbucks either, but he is not *lacking* in the way Angela is. The distinction between existential and formal absence emphasises that non-being does not arise through judgements made by consciousness after encountering the world, but that non-being belongs to the very nature of the world as it is for consciousness. Angela's absence from Starbucks is not merely thought by you. Her absence is an actual event for you that characterises this branch of Starbucks as the place from which Angela is absent.

A person's entire world can exist in the mode of the negative; in the mode of not being the presence of whatever or whoever is desired. The misery of missing someone or something is rooted in this negating of the world. The misery of losing a lover, for example, lies not so much in the loss of the pleasure the lover gave, but in the reduction of the whole world to a dull background that has no other significance or value than to be the perpetual affirmation of the lover's absence. In the fine words of the poet, William Wordsworth:

> I question things, and do not find
> One that will answer to my mind;
> And all the world appears unkind.
> *(The Affliction of Margaret)*

As one further way of showing that the world is shaped by consciousness, consider the phenomenon of *destruction*. Tornados and earthquakes do not destroy, they simply redistribute matter. It is only for a consciousness, for a witness, that entities are destroyed. An earthquake, for example, destroys a city *for us*, because only we can experience the loss of the city as significant. The city has not been destroyed for itself. Human values aside, nothing has been destroyed, in the sense that there is as much matter remaining after an earthquake as there was before.

Destruction requires that there be a witness that is capable of positing the non-being – the *no-longer*-being – of a particular entity. For example, when a cup breaks there is as much china as there was before. Nonetheless, the cup has ceased to be. The requisite cup shape has gone, its capacity to fulfil a certain function has gone. It is these qualities – qualities that have meaning for a consciousness whose projects include drinking – that constitute the being of the cup, not the stuff of which it is made. This is not to say that the qualities can be separated from the stuff. Rearrange the stuff and the qualities become nothing, except, that is, for a consciousness that can 'retain' them in their nothingness in the mode of *was*. A consciousness that can recall the past, compare it to the present and recognise that a particular arrangement no longer exists.

It is high time we explored the existentialist view of time or temporality.

5 Time

The central problematic of all ontology is rooted in the phenomenon of time.
(Martin Heidegger, *Being and Time*, p. 40)

A proper understanding of time or temporality and its very close relationship to consciousness is essential to a proper understanding of existentialism. In a sense, time is the glue that enables the whole theory to hang together; the glue that enables *any* sensible theory of consciousness and the human condition to hang together.

As we've seen, the nature of consciousness is ambiguous and paradoxical. Consciousness is never at one with itself. Indeed, its being is not to be what it is and to be what it is not. Time offers us the best way of making sense of the paradoxical nature of consciousness because we live the paradox of time all the time. We are that paradox. As everyone knows, each of us is continually a past that is no longer and a future that is not yet. Yesterday is just a memory and tomorrow never comes.

It soon becomes quite obvious when you think about it that only an essentially temporal being can have the ambiguous, indefinite, paradoxical nature that consciousness has. Understanding temporality shows how such a nature is possible.

In his major work, *Being and Time*, the German, existentialist philosopher, Martin Heidegger, notes that it is essential to the being of every person that they be situated in the world. Situatedness is a person's essential way of being. Heidegger's term for this essential way of being is *Dasein*.

Quick German lesson coming up. The most common translation of 'Dasein' from the German is 'being-there'. However, although 'sein' certainly means 'being', 'Da' does not always mean 'there'. 'Da' can mean 'neither here nor there, but somewhere in between'. 'Dasein' has been translated as 'being-here', but this formulation is no more exact in that it ignores the 'there' aspect of 'Da'. Quibbling over the exact meaning of 'Da' is useful because it reveals the being of Dasein as that which is neither here nor there. Dasein is essentially indeterminate.

Think of Dasein as being a bit like an object in motion. An object in motion never occupies an exact location. Its exact location at any moment is indeterminate. If it occupied an exact location at any particular moment as it moved then it would be at rest! Therefore, an object in motion must be neither here nor there. A basic understanding of the indeterminate being of Dasein can be gained by comparing it with an object in motion, although this is only an analogy. The essential 'motion' of Dasein – its essential indeterminacy – is not spatial but temporal. Dasein is essentially temporal.

As an essentially temporal movement away from the past towards the future, Dasein temporalises the world. Temporality is the meaning that Dasein gives to the world and is, therefore, the meaning of the world as it is for Dasein. The temporality that Dasein recognises as an essential feature of the world is nothing but its own temporalising of the world – the temporalising that Dasein is. The temporality of the world and the temporality of Dasein are one and the same. Once again, we are back to that rather mind-blowing point made several times in the previous chapter, that consciousness gives rise to time and in doing so shapes the temporal world of our everyday experience.

Although it would be misleading to say that consciousness is temporality, it is nonetheless by virtue of consciousness that the world is temporalised. Time appears in the world through the negation of being that is consciousness. As the negation of being, consciousness must be a perpetual flight, a perpetual escape, from being. But also, as that which strives to be its own negation, consciousness must be a perpetual flight towards being. In short, consciousness endlessly flees being towards being.

Let's put the point in specifically temporal terms that are hopefully less abstract and obscure. Consciousness flees being in the present towards being in the future. If consciousness did not flee being in the present – did not perpetually make the present past – it would coincide with itself in the present. If it coincided with itself in the present it would become a being in itself, and as such would be annihilated as the non-being which it has to be. Hence, consciousness constantly projects itself towards being in the future.

Consciousness, however, can no more coincide with itself in the future than it can coincide with itself in the present. Consciousness cannot coincide with what is not yet, and when the future becomes the present, consciousness, as a perpetual flight from being in the present, will already have flown this new present; will already have made of this new present a past future.

It is important to recognise, as any barroom philosopher will tell you, that there is no such thing as the present. Indeed, there are no such things as the past and the future either. As is widely noted, the past is no longer and the future is not yet. The correct way to view time, then, is not in terms of three distinct and substantial elements – past, present, future – but in terms of three unified dimensions, each of which, being nothing in itself, is outside of itself in the other two and has meaning only in terms of the other two.

Existentialists, convinced that this is how time is, have come up with expressions to help describe it more accurately. As a way of emphasising the intimate relationship between past and future they refer to the future as a *future-past* and to the past as a *past-future*, making the point that in the future the future 'reached' will be the past and as such a past-future. In short, the day after tomorrow, tomorrow will be yesterday.

As for the present, the existentialists note that it is the immediate *presence* of consciousness to being, rather than a present moment that can be considered as being *now*. There is, strictly speaking, no such thing as now. However fast you shout '*Now!*', you succeed only in naming a moment that has passed into the past. As to what is ordinarily described as 'the here and now', it is the situation to which consciousness is presence; the situation that consciousness realises by perpetually surpassing it towards the future.

Consciousness is a flight towards the future. It is a flight that realises the past and the future as its past and future. It is a flight for which the future is a future-past and the past a past-future. It is a flight by which the future becomes the past. There are two immediate conclusions to be drawn from this.

First, being-in-itself is not temporalised. It is only for consciousness which flees it towards the future that being is temporalised. It is only for consciousness that the world, each human situation, is understood as not yet being what it will be and as no longer being what it was. Every situation we find ourselves in has its past and its future written into it by us. My past, so to speak, placed me in this situation, my future is where this situation will lead.

Second, the non-being of the present and the non-being of consciousness are one and the same. The present has no being of its own. The present is not a real or metaphysical condition of the world or the mind but is rather simply the presence of consciousness to the world. As Sartre puts it:

> What is the fundamental meaning of the present? It is clear that what exists in the present is distinguished from all other existence by the characteristic of *presence*. At roll call the soldier or the pupil replies 'Present!' in the sense of *adsum*. *Present* is opposed to *absent* as well as to *past*. Thus the meaning of the *present* is presence to ___. (*Being and Nothingness*, pp. 143–144)

Concluding his argument that the present has precisely the same self-identity-lacking and paradoxical nature as consciousness, or what he calls the for-itself, Sartre re-states his famous maxim that the being of the for-itself is not to be what it is and to be what it is not in specifically temporal terms: 'At present it [the for-itself] is not what it is (past) and it is what it is not (future)' (*Being and Nothingness*, p. 146).

The present is to be equated with consciousness and defined negatively. Equating consciousness with the present and describing it in temporal terms reveals the sense of the apparently absurd claim that consciousness is not what it is and is what it is not. If consciousness was a self-identical positivity, instead of an ambiguous, indeterminate negation, then human reality would be impossible. Experience of the world is possible only for a being that is not like the world, a being that experiences itself as a *relation* to a being that it is not.

As the negation of being, consciousness cannot be co-present with being-in-itself, otherwise its temporal flight would be halted and it would be reduced to being-in-itself. Co-presence – being present at the same time – rather than being the co-presence of consciousness and being-in-itself, is a relationship between physical objects from the point of view of consciousness when consciousness is equally present to them. That lamppost is present to that car *for you* as a presence.

That consciousness cannot be co-present with being implies temporality. As noted, consciousness flees being towards the future. That it does so is an immediate and necessary feature of consciousness. Indeed, consciousness is nothing more than this perpetual flight. The future towards which consciousness flees is the always future possibility of its becoming being-for-itself-in-itself, an always future possibility of fulfilment and completion that is always impossible at present. Consciousness perpetually hankers after this completion without ever being able to achieve it. And it cannot achieve it for the simple reason that the negation of being cannot also be a fullness of being. Consciousness is, and must be, the lack of itself in the present.

Everything said so far about the temporalising of being by consciousness appears to be further evidence for the claim that being is completely undifferentiated apart from consciousness. However, it can be consistently argued both that consciousness temporalises being and that there is a world of distinct phenomena in process apart from consciousness. To argue that there is no time apart from consciousness is not necessarily to argue that apart from consciousness there is no *becoming*; that without consciousness nothing comes into or goes out of existence. It is simply to argue that apart from consciousness there is no *awareness* of the process of becoming; no positing of a past or future for any particular present.

For example, as it is in itself quite apart from anyone being conscious of it, a certain kind of bulb is in process of becoming a daffodil. Yet the bulb is not thereby aiming at becoming a daffodil. It is not projecting itself towards any future goal and has no futurising intentions by means of which it recognises itself as something which presently lacks itself as a daffodil. In the sense that becoming a daffodil is not a project for the bulb, it is correct to say that the bulb has no future. It has a future only for a consciousness that understands that the bulb is not yet a daffodil but will be a daffodil in future

If the claim that there is no time apart from consciousness is understood in this way then it does not amount to an argument against realism – the view that the world is real and exists independently of our consciousness of it. Understood in this way, claiming that there is no time apart from consciousness is not equivalent to claiming that nothing happens apart from consciousness. Rather, it is equivalent to claiming that apart from consciousness the world is without the phenomena of *no-longer* and *not-yet*.

6 Freedom and Choice

Freedom is the freedom of choosing but not the freedom of not choosing.
(Jean-Paul Sartre, *Being and Nothingness*, p. 503)

Existentialists insist that human freedom or free will is not optional. A person does not *choose* to be free. She is free whether she likes it or not because life constantly presents her with the obligation of having to choose between various options, situations and courses of action. This obligation to choose is unavoidable because 'not choosing' is still, in fact, a choice. It is the *choice* not to choose, the *choice* not to take decisive action and so on.

The existentialists argue that each conscious human being is *necessarily free*. Dramatising as usual, Sartre says, 'I am condemned to be free' (*Being and Nothingness*, p. 462); damned to unending freedom by the very fact that I am an ambiguous, indeterminate being existing in a perpetual temporal flight away from the past towards the future. Indeed, it is the existentialists' view of temporality, their firm conviction that human consciousness is essentially temporal, that implies their view that human consciousness is necessarily free.

Human consciousness can never coincide with itself or, to put it another way, unlike tables and chairs a person can never simply be what she is. She is always beyond herself towards the future, always aiming at completion in the future. In a sense a person is her future, but that future is always not-yet. It is in the future at which a person aims that she is free, or rather, she is free in so far as she aims at the future. If a person was simply a fixed entity like a table, something given all at once, then she could not be free. A person possesses a range of possibilities and has options precisely because she is an incomplete being constantly moving towards the future. You cannot have possibilities and options, cannot have freedom, unless you have a future.

Look at it this way. The present is the *presence* of consciousness to the world. As seen, consciousness is nothing in itself; it is nothing in the present. As such, consciousness stands outside the causal order of the physical world. The causal order, that which is, that which cannot be other than it is once it has happened, belongs to a past which consciousness realises by making itself the future of that past. Although the *meaning* of the past can change, the past is fixed in so far as it is that which has been given. However, the past is given to consciousness in terms of the *future possibilities* that consciousness realises for this given past. Indeed, consciousness consists entirely of these future possibilities.

Consciousness is the possibilities of being-in-itself; possibilities that being-in-itself cannot realise for itself but which must be realised for it from the point of view of its negation. Consciousness requires a fixed and given being in order to be that which temporally transcends it towards the future; to be that which renders that being past as it transcends. There is no past except for that which is a flight towards the future and no being towards the future except as a surpassing. As seen, future and past are internally related, they necessarily require one another.

As nothing but a being towards the future, as nothing but the future possibilities of the being of which it is the negation, consciousness has to be these future possibilities. It cannot not be an opening up of possibilities. The freedom of consciousness consists in this perpetual opening up of the possibilities of being, the world, the situation. That is, consciousness continually discovers itself in a world of possibilities which it realises by virtue of its being a temporal surpassing towards the future. If it were not a surpassing, a flight, a transcendence, it would not find itself in a world of possibilities, but rather in a strictly determined world. Of course, as it is nothing but the temporal surpassing of what has been given, it could not exist in such a world.

That which is free – consciousness as a flight towards the future – and that which is not free – being-in-itself that consciousness renders past by surpassing it towards the future – are internally related in that consciousness necessarily requires being-in-itself in order to be a free surpassing of it. This is the all important relationship between what existentialists call *facticity* and *transcendence*.

Facticity is the world around a person in so far as it presents a constant resistance to her actions and projects. Difficulties, obstacles, entanglements, snags, distances, heaviness, instability, fragility, complexity and so on. Yet this constant resistance is the very possibility of a person's actions in that her actions are always a striving to overcome facticity. As Simone de Beauvoir says, 'The resistance of the thing sustains the action of man as air sustains the flight of the dove' (*The Ethics of Ambiguity*, p. 81).

It is only as a free surpassing of facticity that consciousness exists. If there were no facticity to be surpassed and overcome there would be no consciousness. As a free transcendence towards its own future, consciousness necessarily requires something to transcend. Consciousness is, so to speak, perpetually striving to escape from the prison of facticity without ever being able to do so. For consciousness, to be escaping and to be are one and the same. Furthermore, when consciousness escapes to the future it renders the future past as it reaches it, renders it facticity for a further escaping, for a further transcendence.

As seen, it is necessary that consciousness be a free surpassing of being if it is to be at all. This is the *necessity of freedom*. The existence of consciousness is contingent, meaning that it is not necessary, but given that consciousness exists, it is absolutely necessary that it be free. Consciousness is essentially free and it is a necessary condition of its existence that it is not free to cease being free.

Consciousness can never surrender its freedom. It can never render itself an object causally determined by the physical world, for the very project of surrender, the very attempt to render itself causally determined, must be a free choice of itself. Consciousness cannot render itself determined by the world, for whenever or however it attempts to do so, it must *choose* to do so.

We have arrived back where we began at the start of this chapter, making the all important existentialist point that human freedom is not optional. It is not optional because, as Sartre eloquently puts it, 'Freedom is the freedom of choosing but not the freedom of not choosing. Not to choose is, in fact, to choose not to choose' (*Being and Nothingness*, p. 503). An absolute necessity lies at the very heart of human freedom. A person cannot not choose; she cannot not be free; she is condemned to be free.

As a further way of emphasising that people cannot not choose, existentialists are fond of saying that freedom is *unlimited*. This claim has often been misunderstood by critics who take the existentialists to be saying that there is no limit to what a person can choose to do – walk on water, walk through walls, drink the oceans dry. The critics ought to give the existentialists credit for not being quite so stupid and make the effort to understand what it is they actually mean. What the existentialists actually mean when they say freedom is unlimited is that there is no limit, no end, to the responsibility of having to choose a response to every situation. Freedom is unlimited because the obligation to choose is unrelenting.

So, for example, when Sartre famously said, 'I choose to be a cripple' (*Being and Nothingness*, p. 352) – which on the face of it sounds rather politically incorrect – he did not mean that every physically disabled person chooses to have the physical disability that they have. Rather, he meant that a disabled person must choose the meaning of their disability and their response to it, just as an able-bodied person must choose the meaning of their able-bodiedness and their response to it. It is amazing how many disabled people choose to maximise their activity, while so many able-bodied people choose to minimise their activity, but that's another issue.

Disabled people may be pleased to know that in the existentialists' view a physical disability does not limit a person's freedom. Disability is a facticity in face of which a person must constantly choose her own personal path of transcendence. If a person who has lost her legs chooses to give up on everything and sink into inactive resentment of the world, that is no less a choice for which she is responsible than if she chose to pursue some form of positive transcendence not requiring legs – like writing novels, fundraising or winning wheelchair marathons. Do you call this view harsh? Existentialists call it empowering.

The relationship between freedom and facticity is at one with the relationship between consciousness and the world. Freedom is not a capacity of consciousness; freedom is of the very nature of consciousness. Consciousness is free and cannot avoid being so. Freedom is not an essence, just as consciousness is not an essence. Freedom is not a potential that exists prior to being exercised. Freedom is its exercise. Understanding action and choice, therefore, is the key to understanding the existentialist view of freedom.

The defining feature of an action, as distinct from an accidental act, is *intention*. An intention, a chosen end to be realised in the future, gives meaning to the present actions that aim at it and are a means to it. When intentions are realised and ends achieved however, they themselves immediately become means to further ends, with no achieved end ever able to fully and finally satisfy, define and determine a person. As a being that must be a perpetual flight towards the future, a person must always surpass whatever chosen ends she realises for herself towards further chosen ends.

Each word you read here, for example, is surpassed by the sentence, each sentence by the page, each page by the book and so on, with each larger chosen end giving meaning to the complex of actions that serve it. Ultimately, your myriad projects aim at realising an unachievable, godlike state of fulfilment and completion in which you would cease yearning and striving to be at one with yourself and truly *be* at one with yourself.

Each person aims to be at one with herself in her own way. The particular fulfilment and completion at which an individual person aims depends upon her own particular *fundamental choice* of herself; the type of person she chooses herself as. Fundamental choice is considered in detail in Chapter 11 on Children and Childhood. Fundamental choice is a choice by which a person aims to establish herself as a being that is no longer in question. However, as the fundamental choice must be continually affirmed or denied, or possibly abandoned for an alternative fundamental choice, it does not serve to place a person's being beyond question. It remains the case that the nature of a person is to have no nature other than to be a perpetual questioning of her nature. As the existentialists repeatedly argue, human nature is to have no fixed nature or essence. Consider, for example, the nature of cowardice.

The person who chooses to believe she is a coward is likely to live her life seeking to refute this belief. She may perform many brave acts with the intention of overcoming her suspicion. She may even become a heroine in the opinion of others. Yet, for herself, she will remain unable to be at one with the label 'courageous'. However many courageous acts she performs, once performed these acts will sink into her past. Contemplating the future she will say, 'I was courageous, but will I continue to be so? In future battles I fear I will expose my cowardice. I fear I will run away; it is certainly possible.' Equally, she is unable to be at one with the label 'coward' should she try to accept herself as a coward. In attempting to accept herself as a coward doubts would inevitably creep in. It might occur to her that accepting herself as a coward is a courageous thing to do if she must brave the shame of being a coward. Future circumstances might also throw her cowardice into doubt.

Suppose a bully picks once too often on a person who has always considered herself to be a coward and has always acted accordingly.

Suppose the bully finally makes the person so angry that before she has had time to reflect upon her belief in herself as a coward she beats the bully senseless. Following this incident, the person might conclude that her anger temporarily overcame her enduring cowardice. Alternatively, she might conclude that she is not really a coward after all and has been mistaken all her life to think herself a coward.

The ever present possibility of transcending a label in the future necessarily prevents a person from ever permanently attaching a label to herself. To permanently attach a label is, in fact, to have to permanently re-attach it; a necessary condition of the possibility of re-attachment being that the person may choose not to re-attach it. Until she is dead a person can never arrive at a position where re-definition is impossible; a position where she is at one with herself with the possibility of redefining factors excluded. A person is what she has decided to be, but she cannot really *be* it because it is always possible to decide otherwise. Past decisions and past resolutions can always be overturned.

Consider another example. Yesterday, a person decided she would give up drinking alcohol. She redefined herself as teetotal. Today she finds there is nothing to bind her to her decision. Certainly not her determination to quit alcohol, for determination can only ever be based upon a free choice to be determined. Even her doctor's warning that she will die if she continues to hit the gin cannot help her, for she must not only choose to take her doctor's advice into account, she must choose to follow it. If she starts to drink again it does not even necessarily signify that she has dismissed her doctor's advice, for she may respect her doctor's opinion. Rather, it is the case that she is free to ignore good advice even in face of death. Good advice, in itself, has no causal efficacy. Advice may motivate action, but a motive is not an efficient cause.

What, then, can be said of a person who has never drunk alcohol; a person who never gives the possibility of drinking alcohol a serious thought? Surely, she does not perpetually choose herself as drinker or teetotaller? Recalling the existentialist view of lack provides the answer to this question. As seen, when a person chooses a particular course of action she must choose it in terms of a perceived lack.

The person who has never drunk alcohol and never thinks about the possibility of drinking it, as opposed to the drinker who wants to quit or the quitter who wants to resume, does not perceive lacks with regard to drinking alcohol – the lack of a gin or the lack of good health. Rather, she will be concerned with realising herself through the overcoming of other lacks that have nothing whatsoever to do with drinking or not drinking alcohol.

Committed drinkers of alcohol sometimes find it hard to comprehend what they see as the teetotaller's incredible powers of restraint, as though every teetotaller was a former committed drinker actively fighting to maintain their abstinence. Some teetotallers are, of course, former committed drinkers or even reformed alcoholics fighting to maintain their abstinence, but most teetotallers are making no effort at all not to drink alcohol, they simply don't drink it.

These remarks regarding lack suggest that once a person has been a committed drinker of alcohol she will always be a drinker of alcohol; either a drinker who drinks at present or a drinker who does not drink at present. Arguably, even a person who has quit drinking alcohol (so far) continues to be defined in terms of the lack of an alcoholic drink in a way that a person who has never indulged is not defined. For a one-time drinker, lack of alcohol is an existential lack. Alcohol is absent from her life in a way comparable to the absence of an expected friend or enemy. As for the true teetotaller, lack of alcohol is a purely abstract lack. Alcohol is absent from her life in a way comparable to the absence of a stranger who is not expected.

To draw from this consideration of drinkers and non-drinkers what is most important to the view that the self is indeterminate and free, consider the comically irresolute person who can neither accept herself as a drinker nor as a true non-drinker – a drinker who, for example, also chooses herself as another kind of lack to be overcome by good health

One day she will get drunk and worry about her health; the next she will take exercise and find herself looking forward to a bottle of wine at the end of her workout. This predicament will not be due to devil-like desires struggling within her, or even to shame at the weakness of her will, but to a distressing inability that results directly from her freedom to stick to whichever choice she makes. She is unable to stick to whichever choice she makes because she is unable to exercise choice in order to limit, once and for all, her freedom to choose.

The claim that a person cannot not be free sheds light on the nature of commitment. That a person cannot escape the necessity of choice implies that commitment is never a fixed anchor. Indeed it is nothing in itself. Commitment consists entirely in the constant re-affirmation of a certain choice set against the ever present, lurking possibility of a change of mind. Every lover knows this even if they prefer not to think about it.

Anna would have it that Vronsky's love be given freely, for love that is purchased is not love. Yet at the same time, because Anna's happiness depends upon the precarious love of Vronsky, a thought which makes her insecure and not as happy as she expects to be, she wants the love of Vronsky to be a determinate, assured thing; a love-in-itself. However, a love that could not not be given, a love that was not the result of a free choice to love but was simply there, would not be love and as such would be worthless. For more on the existentialist view of love see Chapter 14.

People are defined by what they lack. A person makes sense of herself and her world in terms of what she perceives to be presently lacking. A person always perceives her situation as lacking something. However, as situations do not lack anything in themselves, whatever the situation of a person lacks must, in fact, be a lack for that person. In short, a person introduces lack into her situation.

What a situation lacks constitutes the future possibilities of that situation. Therefore, the future possibilities of a situation – by virtue of which it is a situation – are really nothing but the future possibilities of a person in that situation. A situation is never its own situation, it is always a situation for, and the situation of, a person. The nature, meaning and value that a situation has is bestowed upon it by the person for whom it is a situation.

The nature, meaning and value of a hill, for example, depends upon the freely chosen ends of the person who encounters it. If the projected end goal of the person is to climb the hill, then the hill will manifest itself in the situation of that person as easy to climb, difficult to climb or insurmountable. The exact details of how the hill manifests itself will depend on further factors relating to the person. How determined she is, how healthy she is, her skill as a climber and the tools she has at her disposal. Perhaps it is only a small hill, but small hills are not so small if one is disabled or wearing high heel shoes.

The way in which these factors affect the situation depends in large part upon previous choices that a person has made. Her ability as a climber will largely be a result of past decisions to take regular exercise. Her overall determination in the past and at present in face of the hill will reveal her choice of herself as dogged or defeatist. On the other hand, the person who has no intention of climbing the hill will, if she notices it at all, view it only as an aesthetic object that she finds pretty or ugly.

Finally, as a way of further supporting the existentialists' claim that a person cannot not be free, it is worth noting that choosing a particular course of action always involves not choosing another course of action that could have been chosen. Unless a person has, for example, been reduced to a mere object by falling off a cliff, there are always alternative courses of action that she can take.

When a person says, for example, 'I have no choice but to act this way,' she ignores the fact that she can choose to do nothing. This is not to suggest that inaction is always a sensible option, just that it is always a possible option. If someone says they will kill a person's family if she does not cooperate, she is not thereby causally determined to cooperate! She can still choose not to. The decision to cooperate is still her choice.

The notion of *compulsion*, as applied in law, for example, still makes sense despite this claim. The notion of compulsion can be understood in the following way. To say that a person was *compelled* is to say that she *chose* to do what any rational person would do if severely threatened. Similarly, when people say, 'I can do nothing,' they ignore the fact that they can always choose to do something, even if all they can do for the time being is plot how they might escape from their real or metaphorical chains.

7 Anxiety and Vertigo

Hence anxiety is the dizziness of freedom. (Søren Kierkegaard, *The Concept of Anxiety*, p. 61)

Fear and anxiety. Ordinarily, these terms are used interchangeably, or anxiety is seen as a species of fear, perhaps the kind of creeping fear that is experienced when what is feared has not yet become clear and present – anxiety as a prelude to fear. 'The people were *anxious* there would be a bombing raid.' 'The people cowered in *fear* as the bombs fell.' Existentialists, however, draw a clear distinction between fear and anxiety, although they see them as related in various ways.

As far as existentialists are concerned, fear must be distinguished from what they call *existential anxiety*, *angst, anguish* or *dread*. For existentialists, fear is a person's concern about what threatens her from outside, the myriad threats to life, limb, livelihood and happiness that she has little or no control over. 'The heart-ache and the thousand natural shocks that flesh is heir to' (Shakespeare, *Hamlet*, Act 3, Scene 1). Anxiety, on the other hand, is a person's concern about what, so to speak, threatens her from inside. She is concerned about what she might choose to do given her unlimited freedom to do it. An anxious person is troubled by her own freedom and spontaneity, by her awareness that there is nothing whatsoever preventing her from choosing to perform a foolish, destructive or disreputable act other than her choice, her freedom, not to perform it

The existentialist preoccupation with anxiety began with Kierkegaard and a book he wrote called *The Concept of Anxiety*. In that book
Kierkegaard takes the example of a man standing on the edge of a tall
building or cliff. The man fears he might fall over the edge, that the
safety rail or the ground might give way, that someone might push him
off and so on. But greater than his fear of falling is his anxiety that he
can choose to jump, that he is free to jump if he decides to. Anxiety in
this context is called *vertigo*.

During vertigo the drop obsesses us, the void seems to beckon us
down, but really it is our own freedom that beckons us down, the very
fact that we can always choose to go down the quick way! Vertigo is
dread of this alarming and persistent possibility, and all our alarming
possibilities produce in us a psychological state akin to vertigo. Not
surprisingly, Sartre calls the anxiety we experience whenever we
consider dangerous experiments in freedom the 'vertigo of possibility'
(*The Transcendence of the Ego*, p. 100).

What a person overlooking a sheer drop dreads is not the void
yawning below her immediately beyond the physical guard rail, but
that she ultimately lacks an inner psychological guard rail to prevent
her from choosing to climb over the physical guard rail and plunge to
her death. If it appears on the face of it that her dread is of the void
itself this is because her vivid awareness of the void immediately forces
her to confront her dreadful possibilities in relation to it. The void is the
occasion of her dread but not its source.

Interestingly, if the woman fancies she has a fixed inner psychological guard rail that prevents her from choosing to jump then she is
deluding herself because whatever psychological barrier she possesses
is merely a flimsy construct of her freedom. It is a barrier consisting of
nothing more than the choice not to jump, a choice that she is free to
replace at any moment with the choice to jump. Her anxiety is precisely
her awareness of the ease with which she can spontaneously overturn
the chosen self-determinations that she wishes would permanently fix,
define, preserve and protect her.

The flimsy, inner, psychological guard rails that we continually construct out of our freedom do, in effect, help keep us on the straight and narrow. We work hard to convince ourselves that these guard rails are real and independent entities, features of our prudent character or our naturally cautious nature and so on. They serve as guard rails against anxiety in general, as comforting smoke screens put up by freedom through which freedom does not see itself as starkly as it otherwise might.

If the woman on the cliff edge focuses, for example, on what she likes to believe is her strong instinct for survival, then she distracts herself from the thought that she is free to jump and the anxiety that goes with that thought. All such self-distraction and self-evasion, all such faith in inner guard rails, freedom-limiting factors and fixed personal characteristics is what existentialists call *bad faith*. A degree of bad faith appears vital for sustaining well-being and even sanity. Even so, existentialists tend to despise bad faith. Bad faith is explored in detail in the next chapter.

The example of the anxious person on the tall building or cliff has become famous in existentialist circles, not least because it has been reformulated by various existentialist philosophers that came after Kierkegaard, most notably Sartre. Sartre embroiders Kierkegaard's example by imagining himself walking along a narrow precipice path without a guard rail (*Being and Nothingness*, pp. 54–56). Sartre and de Beauvoir liked to go on walking holidays in the Alps and the Pyrenees and it is clear that Sartre is writing from first-hand experience. He argues that although his vertigo is not fear of falling, it initially announces its onset through fear as he finds himself reflecting on all the circumstances that could cause him to fall over the edge. He begins to take evasive action. He keeps as far away from the edge as possible and watches where he puts his feet. He shapes his conduct according to a motive of survival.

However, in adopting this motive it becomes increasingly clear to him as he moves forward that he must keep on re-adopting it without there being any guarantee that he will do so. He rapidly becomes anxious about his future conduct, his future self. What if he loses concentration or decides to run? What if his future self abandons the motive of survival that has preserved him until now and he decides instead to jump? It *is* possible, and it is his dread of that possibility, dread of his future self and his inability to determine its choices, that constitutes his vertigo. Sartre writes:

> If *nothing* compels me to save my life, *nothing* prevents me from precipitating myself over the abyss. The decisive conduct will emanate from a self which I am not yet. Thus the self which I am depends on the self which I am not yet to the exact extent that the self which I am not yet does not depend on the self which I am. Vertigo appears as the apprehension of this dependence. (*Being and Nothingness*, p. 56)

Vertigo is a person's anxious realisation that she cannot trust her future self. To take another of Sartre's examples, a man going to war is likely to fear injury and death, but he is more likely to suffer anxiety as he reflects on the personal trials ahead. 'Present fears are less than horrible imaginings' (Shakespeare, *Macbeth*, Act 1, Scene 3). Can he trust himself to hold it all together, to conduct himself with dignity and avoid behaving like a coward? A recruit 'can in some instances be afraid of death, but more often he is "afraid of being afraid;" that is, he is filled with anguish before himself' (*Being and Nothingness*, p. 53).

A further example of anxiety as a lack of trust in what one might choose to do next is attributed by Sartre to the French philosopher and writer, Paul Janet. Retelling Janet's story in one of his earliest works Sartre writes:

> A young bride was in terror, when her husband left her alone, of sitting in the window and summoning passers-by like a prostitute. Nothing in her education, in her past, nor in her character could serve as an explanation of such a fear. It seems to us simply that a negligible circumstance (reading, conversation, etc.) had determined in her what might be called a 'vertigo of

possibility'. She found herself monstrously free, and this vertiginous freedom appeared to her *at the opportunity* for this action which she was afraid of doing. (*Transcendence of the Ego*, p. 100)

It seems the young bride needs to convince herself that she is not as free as she in fact is. She needs to fool herself that she has a fixed self that is incapable of doing such scandalous things, a self that can be trusted because it will be the same in future as it is now. In short, she is in need of a healthy dose of bad faith. Bad faith can protect a person's social standing from dangerous experiments in freedom. The young bride is in desperate need of bad faith to prevent her from succumbing to the vertigo of possibility. Bad faith will spare her the anguish of even contemplating acting with impropriety. As said, bad faith can protect the psychological well-being of a person by serving as a guard rail against anxiety. More on bad faith shortly.

Existentialist writers, perhaps for dramatic effect, perhaps for ease of explanation, have tended to focus on anxiety experienced in face of the dangerous or foolish act that nothing but a person's own freedom prevents her from doing. But anxiety can also be experienced in face of the sensible act that nothing but her own freedom makes her do. She is anxious because she could choose to jump through the window to her death, but she is also anxious because she could choose not to wash herself, eat properly or pay her bills. Small anxieties no doubt, but there are very many occasions for such small anxieties amongst the complexity of modern life and so the anxieties stack up to a whole heap of stress.

Perhaps in the end not choosing to do a sensible thing is choosing to do a foolish thing, so the distinction is more or less irrelevant. Nonetheless, attempting to make the distinction does seem to highlight a far wider range of occasions for anxiety. Moreover, it appears to support what common sense suggests: that a person is not normally anxious that she could choose to jump out of her window, anymore than she is anxious about all the other self-destructive things she could do that she hasn't even thought of. But that a person is constantly anxious to a lesser or greater extent about always having to decide what *for her* is sensible, foolish, worthwhile, pointless, valuable, no longer valuable and so on, and about always having to pick and choose a path through life accordingly.

8 Bad Faith

Here we find a pattern of *distraction*. (Jean-Paul Sartre, *Being and Nothingness*, p. 77)

Human consciousness is essentially free; a free flight or transcendence towards the future. Bad faith is a direct possibility of human freedom because bad faith always involves a person *choosing* herself as a being that need not or cannot make choices, as a being that need not or cannot take responsibility for her responses to situations. Bad faith is the exercise of freedom against itself, it is freedom seeking to deny itself. If, as we have seen, people are inalienably free, then a person in bad faith must be fooling herself somehow. She must be placing faith in an illusion of herself that is contrary to her true nature, an illusion that she herself creates and sustains moment by moment.

It is tempting to say that she *deceives* herself and that bad faith is self-deception, and this is certainly what bad faith appears to be at first glance. Existentialists, however, resist labelling bad faith as self-deception because self-deception as such is impossible.

It is not possible for a person to lie to herself in the way that she can lie to another person. The other person, being other, has no direct access to her consciousness. There is a duality of consciousnesses. One consciousness can know what the other consciousness does not know and can therefore deceive the other consciousness. There is, however, no such duality within the unity of a single consciousness, otherwise it would not be a *single* consciousness. A person cannot attempt to deceive herself as she deceives another person without instantly catching herself in the act.

A person can hope to get away with sneaking a piece of the board when she is playing another person at checkers, for example, but she cannot hope to get away with cheating if she is playing herself at checkers. She will always catch herself in the act of deception. Indeed, she will catch herself so readily in her very *intention* to deceive, that such an intention cannot be seriously formed. It is because a person cannot conceal *any* intention from herself when playing herself at checkers, either within the rules or not within the rules, that a person only ever plays herself at checkers as an exploration of the impossibility of *really* playing herself at checkers.

Far from being self-deception, bad faith is rather a form of *self-distraction* or *self-evasion*. The term 'deception' suggests a liar, but consider the way a conjuror deceives us. The hand is quicker than the eye because the conjurer employs techniques to distract us. The person in bad faith deliberately strives to avoid certain truths by distracting herself from them, by *ignoring* them.

Although the term 'ignorance' is often used to describe the disposition of *not knowing*, ignorance is in fact a form of knowing. Jane can only *ignore* Peter if she knows he is there. To ignore someone is to know they are there, yet at the same time to behave, or try to behave, as though they are not there. A person who ignores another is not *deceiving* herself that the other person is not there, rather she is pretending she is in a world in which the other person is not there. A person, a lover for example, may want the presence of another so she can attract his interest by ignoring him. At other times, however, to strive to ignore someone is to strive in vain to be in an alternative reality where that person does not exist.

In a similar way, a person in bad faith strives to ignore her indeterminacy, ambiguity, freedom and responsibility. She strives in vain to enter an idealised alternative reality where she is a fixed entity that is no longer obliged to make choices, to act, to take responsibility for her present situation. An idealised alternative reality where the lifelong burden of freedom and responsibility can be relinquished is what the person in bad faith aims at and preoccupies herself with.

She aims at this idealised alternative reality in a future that presents itself as realisable and about to be realised but that can never in fact be reached precisely because it can only exist in the future. Rather than *confront* her present situation, rather than choose herself responsibly as the transcendence of her present circumstances, she chooses herself irresponsibly as (about to be) the transcendence of herself. She aims at being entirely detached from what she is – a person who must choose what she is and must take responsibility for what she chooses – by striving to be a pure transcendence rather than the transcendence of her facticity.

To make better sense of the above abstractions we need to look at specific, concrete examples of people in bad faith. After all, bad faith is not an abstract concept but a concrete, existential phenomenon; the attitude, disposition and way of behaving of particular persons in particular situations. To examine concrete examples of people in bad faith is certainly Sartre's approach to explaining the phenomenon. As the existentialist theory of bad faith is largely Sartre's theory, exploring his most notable examples of people in bad faith is undoubtedly the best way forward.

Famous among Sartre's examples of people in bad faith is the flirtatious but naïve young woman (*Being And Nothingness*, pp. 78–79). The flirt is approached by a guy who clearly fancies her. She takes the guy's compliments and polite attentions at face value ignoring their sexual undercurrent. Finally, he takes her hand, establishing a situation that demands from her a decisive response. But she chooses to flirt, neither withdrawing her hand nor acknowledging the implications of holding hands. She treats her hand as though it is not a part of herself, as though it is an object for which she is not responsible, and she treats her act of omission of leaving her hand in the hand of the guy as though it is not an action.

The flirt knows her hand is held and what this implies yet somehow she evades this knowledge, or rather she is the ongoing project of seeking to evade it and distract herself from it. She distracts herself from the meaning of her situation and the disposition of her limbs by fleeing herself towards the future. Each moment she aims to become a being beyond her situated self, the meaning of which would not be her current situation. She aims to become a being that is what it is, an object. Such a being would not be subject to the demands of the situation. It would not be obliged to choose and to act.

She abandons her hand, her whole body, to the past, hoping to leave it all behind her. Yet, in the very act of abandoning it, she re-apprehends the situation of her body as a demand to choose. To take the man's hand willingly or to withdraw, that is the choice. But she fails to meet this demand by choosing herself as a person that would-be beyond the requirement to choose. It is this negative choice that exercises and distracts her and stands in for the positive choice she knows her situation demands. She avoids making this positive choice by striving to choose herself as a person who has transcended her responsibility for her embodied, situated self. She strives to choose herself as a being that has escaped its facticity.

Every human being is both an object and a subject, a facticity and a transcendence, or to be more precise, the transcendence *of* her facticity. There are various related forms of bad faith as revealed by the various concrete examples Sartre provides and all of them manipulate in some way the subject-object 'double property of the human being' (*Being and Nothingness*, p. 79). Essentially, bad faith is the project of seeking to invert and/or separate facticity and transcendence.

The flirt treats the facticity of her situation, in terms of which her choices of herself should be exercised, as though it has a transcendent power over her body. That is, she treats her facticity as though it is a transcendence. At the same time, she treats her transcendent consciousness as though it is its own transcendence; as though it is a transcendence-in-itself rather than the transcendence of the facticity of her situation. That is, she treats her transcendence as though it is a facticity.

Another of Sartre's examples of a character in bad faith is the waiter (*Being and Nothingness*, pp. 82–83). Sartre paints a vivid picture of the waiter in action. The waiter walks with a robotic stiffness, restraining his movements as though he were a machine. He steps a little too rapidly towards his customers, he is a little too eager and attentive. He is playing at being a waiter.

One view of Sartre's waiter is that he is in bad faith for striving, through his performance, to deny his transcendence and become his facticity. He overacts his role as a waiter in order to convince himself and others that he is a waiter-*thing*. As a waiter-*thing* he would escape his freedom and the anxiety it causes him. He aims to become *for himself* the mere function that he often is for others in his role as waiter. He strives to be at one with his own representation of himself, but the very fact that he has to represent to himself what he is means that he cannot be it.

Striving to be a thing so as to escape the responsibility of being free is certainly an identifiable form of bad faith. However, against this view of Sartre's waiter, it can be argued that although the waiter does indeed strive to be a waiter-*thing*, he is not in bad faith because the purpose of his striving is not to escape his freedom. Arguably, he is no more in bad faith for striving to be a waiter than an actor is in bad faith for striving to be Macbeth.

A closer reading of Sartre's description of the waiter reveals that, just like an actor, there is a definite sense in which he knows what he is doing. He acts with ironical intent, consciously – though not self-consciously – impersonating a waiter. It is a good impersonation that has become second nature to him. To claim that acting like a waiter is second nature to him is not to claim that he believes he has become a waiter. Rather, it is to claim that he has become his performance in the sense that when he is absorbed in it he does not reflect that he is performing. Sartre says that the waiter 'plays with his condition in order to *realize* it' (*Being and Nothingness*, p. 82). He does not mean that the waiter plays with his condition in order to become it, but that his condition is only ever realised as a playing with his condition. As it is impossible for any conscious being to achieve identity with itself, the waiter can never *be* what he is. He can only play at being it.

It can be argued that, far from being in bad faith, the waiter is *authentic*, the very antithesis of bad faith. Unlike the flirt he does not evade what he is, the transcendence *of* his facticity, by striving to treat his facticity as a transcendence and his transcendence as a facticity. Instead, he strives to take full responsibility for the reality of his situation, choosing himself positively in his situation by throwing himself wholeheartedly into his chosen role. He strives to embrace what existentialists call his *being-in-situation*. A waiter in bad faith would be a reluctant, rueful waiter; a waiter who thought, 'I am not really a waiter'; a waiter who chose to wait at tables while wishing he were someone else somewhere else. Authenticity is considered in detail in Chapter 10.

Sartre's example of the homosexual (*Being and Nothingness*, pp. 86–88) reveals further important dimensions of the phenomenon of bad faith. The homosexual does not deny his homosexual desires and activities. Instead, he denies that homosexuality is the meaning of his conduct. Rather than take responsibility for his conduct he chooses to characterise it as a series of aberrations, as the result of curiosity rather than the result of a deep-seated tendency and so on. He believes that a homosexual is not a homosexual as a chair is a chair.

This belief is justified in so far as a person is never what he is but only what he aims to be through his choices. The homosexual is right that he is not a homosexual-*thing*, but in so far as he has adopted conduct defined as the conduct of a homosexual, he is a homosexual. That he is not a homosexual in the sense that a chair is a chair does not imply that he is not a homosexual in the sense that a chair is not a table. The homosexual plays around with the word 'being'. He slyly interprets 'not being what he *is*', as 'not being what he is not'.

The homosexual attempts to deny he is his facticity, when, in fact, he is his facticity in the mode of no longer being it. That is, although he is not his facticity – his past – in the mode of being it, he is his facticity in so far as it is a past that he affirms as his by having to continually transcend it towards the future. He assumes in bad faith that he is a pure transcendence, that his facticity, being past, has vanished into the absolute nothingness of a generalised past that has nothing whatsoever to do with him. In truth, far from being a pure transcendence, he is and must be the transcendence of his facticity. In his project of bad faith the homosexual attempts to create within himself a rift between facticity and transcendence.

The homosexual has a friend, a champion of sincerity, who urges him to come out and admit that he is a homosexual. In doing so, he urges him to consider himself a facticity rather than a pure transcendence. In urging the homosexual to consider himself a facticity the champion of sincerity aims to stereotype him as 'just a homosexual'. It is easier for him to achieve this aim if he can persuade the homosexual to apply the label 'homosexual' to himself. His motive in seeking to stereotype the homosexual is to deny him the freedom that makes him an individual; it is to transcend him, to label him, to get the better of him.

Ordinarily, sincerity is seen as a form of honesty or good faith. Sartre, however, exposes sincerity as a form of bad faith. If the homosexual took his friend's advice to be sincere and admitted he was a homosexual, if he declared, 'I am what I am', he would not overcome his bad faith. He would simply exchange the bad faith of considering himself a pure transcendence for the bad faith of considering himself a facticity.

We have already seen that the person who considers herself a facticity is in bad faith for seeking to evade the truth that she is the transcendence *of* her facticity. To declare 'I am what I am' is to assert the fallacy that I am a fixed entity, while at the same time evading the existential truth that I am an indeterminate being who must continually create myself through choice and action. In short, it is to declare myself a facticity when in reality I am the transcendence of my facticity.

The sincerity identified above is relatively unsophisticated. Sartre also identifies a more sophisticated and devious form of sincerity. This more sophisticated form of sincerity still involves a person declaring 'I am what I am', but here her aim is not to be what she is, rather it is to distance herself from what she is through the very act by which she declares what she is.

In declaring herself to be a thing she aims to become that which declares she is a thing rather than the thing she declares herself to be. She posits herself as a thing in order to escape being that thing; in order to become that which contemplates the thing she has ceased to be. Unlike a person who adopts the simpler form of sincerity, she does not aim to be her facticity by denying her transcendence, she aims to be a pure transcendence divorced from her facticity. Sartre identifies *confession* as an instance of this more sophisticated form of sincerity.

The person who confesses a sin, for example, renders her sin into an object for her contemplation that exists only in so far as she contemplates it and ceases to exist when she ceases to contemplate it. Believing herself to be a pure transcendence she believes she is free to move on from her sin and to abandon it to the past as a disarmed sin that is neither her possession nor her responsibility. Confession that aims at absolution is bad faith.

In *Truth and Existence* Sartre takes the example of a woman with tuberculosis (*Truth and Existence*, pp. 33–35). The woman refuses to acknowledge that she has tuberculosis despite having all the symptoms. She views each symptom in isolation, refusing to recognise their collective meaning. She engrosses herself in pursuits that do not afford her time to visit the doctor, pursuits that distract her from making the choices required by her situation. Her symptoms place her at the threshold of new knowledge, but she chooses ignorance because she does not want the responsibility of dealing with her tuberculosis, of seeking a cure for it and so on, that new knowledge would call for. In her refusal to face her situation, in her self-distraction and her evasion of responsibility, she is similar to Sartre's flirt considered earlier.

Bad faith is wilful ignorance. Bad faith is irresponsibility. To dispense with such wilful ignorance and irresponsibility and instead to courageously affirm the hard existential truths of the human condition – ambiguity, freedom, responsibility, mortality and so on – is to overcome bad faith in favour of authenticity. It is nearly time to examine the existential holy grail of authenticity, but first we need to examine *responsibility*, the raw material from which that holy grail is made.

9 Responsibility

> In the long run, we shape our lives and we shape ourselves. The process
> never ends until we die. And the choices we make are ultimately our own
> responsibility. (Eleanor Roosevelt, *You Learn by Living*, Foreword)

'Responsibility to me is tragedy.' So sang Sister Sledge ('Lost in Music'),
expressing what most people feel most of the time, that responsibility
is a burden they wish they could escape. Existentialists also recognise
that responsibility is a burden, but their hard-nosed view is that responsibility is a burden people should learn to relish as it is not a burden they
can ever abandon.

Sure, people can downshift, or avoid shifting up in the first place. Get
a job where they have less *responsibilities* in the sense of having less
people placing constant pressure on them to make difficult decisions and
complete complex tasks. But in existentialist terms, to stick near the bottom
of the professional or social ladder is not to escape the burden of responsibility. This is because what existentialists understand by responsibility is
somewhat different from what is ordinarily understood by responsibility.

Ordinarily, people equate responsibility with a person's responsibilities and obligations, the things they are obliged to do to put food on
the table and keep the wolf from the door. When existentialists talk
about responsibility they tend to mean *self-responsibility*, a person's
responsibility for their own inalienable freedom, for the choices they
make and the actions they take.

An existentialist will accept that in the ordinary way of speaking a head teacher probably has more responsibilities than one of the people who clean her school, but the existentialist will insist that both the head teacher and the cleaner are equally responsible for who they are, for what they do and don't do and for the path they steer through life generally. Both cleaner and head teacher have to make decisions all the time, not least in the world beyond the mere job they choose to do, and they are equally burdened with, and equally responsible for, the decisions they make and the person those decisions create.

To fully grasp the existentialist view of responsibility we have to begin by re-stating what is perhaps the central maxim of existentialism, namely, that human consciousness is not a fixed, determined entity. There is nothing that a person is or can be in the mode of being it. A person must continually create herself in response to her situation through the choices she makes. A person cannot not choose herself in response to her situation because not to choose is in fact a choice not to choose.

In other words, the only limit to a person's freedom is that she is not free to cease being free. As her responses to her situation are always chosen, she is responsible for them. As said, she is burdened with the responsibility of her freedom. Now, a person is not always responsible for her situation, for her facticity, but in so far as she must choose her responses to her situation, and in so doing choose herself in her situation, she is obliged to *assume* responsibility for her situation, obliged to *take on* her situation.

A disabled person, for example, may well not be responsible for bringing about her disability, but she is nonetheless responsible for her disability in the sense that she is free to choose her response to it and decide upon its meaning. If she decides that it is the ruination of her life then that is her choice, her responsibility. When looking specifically at freedom and choice in Chapter 6, I noted Sartre's provocative claim that a person chooses to be a cripple. Sartre does not mean to be offensive here but to emphasise the point that disabled people, though they do not possess the freedom of movement able-bodied people possess, nonetheless possess unlimited freedom when it comes to deciding what being disabled means to them and how they will deal with the facticity, the brute fact, of their disability.

To insist that a disabled person is, existentially speaking, responsible for her disability, is certainly a tough and uncompromising view. It even seems a harsh and politically incorrect view in a culture that consistently undervalues individual responsibility and consistently overvalues the blaming of circumstances and facticity. This view should, however, be seen as empowering and very much politically correct in terms of the respect it shows disabled people.

To tell a so-called disabled person that she is, existentially speaking, responsible for her disability, is not to insult her or show her a callous lack of consideration, it is to inspire her and offer her genuine hope. Any disabled person whose choice of herself is not to wallow in self-pity would surely embrace this description of her situation. Few disabled people want to be reduced to their disability; considered as just a broken thing in a wheelchair. The existentialists are saying precisely that a disabled person is not her disability but instead her freely chosen response to her disability and her transcendence of it. This realisation is, or should be, enormously empowering. Personal empowerment is right at the top of the existentialists' responsibility agenda.

It is important to note that bad faith, as a choice not to choose, is above all else an attempt to evade or relinquish responsibility. In the previous chapter we met Sartre's flirt and Sartre's homosexual. These two characters represent two forms of bad faith, both of which aim at avoiding responsibility. Sartre's flirt attempts to avoid taking responsibility for her present actions and the demands of her immediate situation, while Sartre's homosexual attempts to avoid taking responsibility for his past deeds.

Another form of bad faith in which a person attempts to avoid taking responsibility is sincerity. A sincere person, a person who makes a confession for example, declares, 'I am what I am,' in order to instantly abandon what she is to the past. In reality she is the transcendence of the facticity of her past, and as such is responsible for her past, but she aims at separating her facticity and her transcendence, her past and her future, so as to become a pure transcendence in a virgin future where she has escaped what she was and is no longer responsible for it.

Authenticity, as the antithesis of bad faith, involves a person taking full responsibility for herself, her past and her situation without blame, excuse or regret. Rather than seeking to deny the reality of her situation, the authentic person acts positively and decisively to meet the demands of her situation without complaint; without wishing she was not responsible for meeting the demands of her situation.

To embrace and celebrate being responsible is to embrace and celebrate being free. Freedom is not freedom from responsibility, freedom is having to make choices and therefore having to take responsibility. The person in bad faith, the inauthentic person, seeks to avoid recognising that one of the fundamental existential truths of her existence is that she is free and responsible, whereas the authentic person not only recognises that she is free and responsible, she strives to come to terms with it and to treat it as an ultimate value. Responsibility is certainly not a tragedy for the authentic person.

The theory of radical freedom and responsibility put forward by such hard-line existentialists as de Beauvoir and Sartre has been criticised as too uncompromising by more moderate existentialists such as Merleau-Ponty. Merleau-Ponty and his clique argue that there are limitations to freedom; that people do not always choose their responses to their situation and are therefore not always responsible for their actions. One of their main arguments is that each person has a *natural self* based on the natural limitations of her body.

This natural self renders certain evaluations inevitable and disposes a person towards certain choices. In failing to acknowledge that a person's interactions with the world and other people are pre-structured by a natural self, the hard-line existentialists also overlook various behavioural and dispositional phenomena that signify limitations to choice and responsibility. Among the phenomena that the critics identify are sense of humour, sexual preference and mental disturbance.

Examining these phenomena reveals that perhaps not every conscious response is freely chosen. Although education and experience may change a person's sense of humour over time, if she finds a joke funny at the time she hears it she is not choosing to find it funny. Similarly, although a sane person is responsible for actions that stem from her sexual preferences she is not responsible for her sexual preferences. She does not choose them and cannot choose to change them. Finally, psychiatrists recognise that the genuinely mentally disturbed have obsessive, compulsive tendencies over which they have little or no control. The radical freedom and responsibility theory of the hard-liners does not allow for the *diminished responsibility* that is one of the central features of insanity.

The hard-line existentialists are right that responsibility cannot be avoided or freedom limited by choosing not to choose. They are also right that helplessness in many if not most life situations is a pathetic pretence. They appear, however, to be wrong that people are always responsible for what they do and the evaluations they make.

Perhaps, in the end, the hard-line existentialists are not offering us a philosophical theory worked out in every single detail, so much as an ideal to aspire to through sheer unrelenting willpower – a dignified life of maximum responsibility and minimum excuses. Or, like so many people in our decadent, undignified western culture, would you rather aspire to be a whinging, irresponsible waster?

10 Authenticity

The highest men act out their lives without keeping back any residue of inner experience. (Friedrich Nietzsche, *Human, All-too-Human* Volume 2, *Assorted Opinions and Maxims*, 228)

One thing that can be said with certainty about authenticity is that it is the opposite of bad faith. Bad faith is synonymous with inauthenticity. Authenticity is also distinct from sincerity which, as we have seen, is a form of bad faith. Previous chapters have hopefully made it clear that the most blatant feature of all forms of inauthenticity is the attempted evasion of responsibility. Certainly, all the characters in bad faith we've looked at are seeking to evade responsibility in one way or another.

Inauthentic people maintain particular projects of avoiding responsibility for their present situation or their past deeds by refusing, in bad faith, to acknowledge that they *are* responsible. More specifically, they refuse to acknowledge their inability to be a fixed entity, their unlimited freedom and the implications of their unlimited freedom. Recall that every consciousness, as nothing but the negation of being-in-itself, is founded upon what it is not. It cannot, therefore, become its own foundation or coincide with itself. There is nothing that a person can be without having to make herself be it. Unable to be what she is, a person must perpetually *choose* what she is by choosing her responses to situations. She cannot not choose to respond to situations, and because her responses are chosen she is responsible for them. Even if her response is to do nothing, that is still a choice for which she is responsible.

In the existentialists' view, inauthenticity is the denial of the cardinal truth that we are free and responsible, whereas authenticity, as the antithesis of inauthenticity, is the acceptance or affirmation of this cardinal truth. Existentialists argue that authenticity involves a person confronting reality and facing up to the hard truth that she is a limitlessly free being who will never obtain coincidence with herself. Whereas the inauthentic person seeks to avoid recognising that this is the fundamental truth of her being, the authentic person not only recognises it, she strives to come to terms with it, affirm it and even to treat it as a source of values. The authentic person responds fully to the appeal to face up to reality that pervades existentialism.

As a radical conversion that involves a person affirming what in truth she has always been – a free and responsible being lacking coincidence with herself – adopting human reality as her own does not involve a radical change of being. Rather, it involves a radical shift in her attitude towards herself and her unavoidable *situatedness*. Instead of exercising her freedom in order to deny her freedom, instead of choosing not to choose, the authentic person *assumes* her freedom, acknowledges it, takes it on board, gets with it.

Assuming her freedom involves assuming full responsibility for herself in whatever situation she happens to find herself. It involves accepting that this and no other is her situation; that this situation is the facticity in terms of which she must now choose herself. If she is not imprisoned she can, of course, reject her situation by running away, but this still involves a choice. A choice that gives rise to new situations and to new demands to choose. Above all, assuming her freedom involves realising that because she is nothing in the mode of being it she is nothing but the choices she makes in her situation.

Imagine a guy called Steve who has lived as a civilian for many years. One day Steve gets his call-up papers and reluctantly joins the army. Steve is now a soldier. True, he is not a soldier in the manner of being a soldier-*thing*, but in so far as he wears a uniform and fights in an army 'soldier' is the meaning of his conduct. Remembering his years as a civilian, Steve inauthentically insists that he is not a soldier but a civilian *disguised* as a soldier. In saying this, Steve reveals that he is not taking responsibility for his choices. He makes himself something by acting in a certain way, while at the same time trying to run away from it and deny it.

Steve flees what he is making of himself – a soldier – towards the non-existent civilian-*thing* that he mistakenly fancies himself to be. He has not accepted what Sartre, who wrote about this kind of inauthenticity in his *War Diaries*, calls his *being-in-situation*. In denying that he is only ever his responses to his facticity, Steve pleads the excuse of his facticity. He chooses to see himself as a facticity, as a given, fixed entity swept along by circumstances.

It is in ceasing to be like Steve and accepting her being-in-situation that a person ceases to think of herself as swept along by circumstances and becomes authentic. An authentic person looks honestly and realistically at what the present situation requires, what constitutes a responsible attitude and responsible actions in that situation, then embraces that situation without regret. She throws herself wholeheartedly into it; into dealing with it and making the most of it.

If you've seen that great Vietnam war movie, *Apocalypse Now*, then you may be inclined to agree that this is the attitude of Lieutenant Colonel William Kilgore – the guy who loves the smell of napalm in the morning. Is Kilgore crazy, evil, a murderer? Maybe he's all three, but as is said in the film, 'Charging a man with murder in this place was like handing out speeding tickets at the Indy 500.' Kilgore is no more crazy, evil and murderous than the war situation in which he finds himself, a situation into which he has utterly plunged himself, not just 'making the most of it' but positively relishing it.

Under the terms of conventional morality, Kilgore is a monster; under the terms of existentialism he is honest and authentic because his situation *demands a monster*. Would he be a better man if he did what he does indecisively, remorsefully, dishonestly? Would he be a better man if he pathetically appeased his guilt by blaming circumstances and other people, all the while striving for some dubious moral justification? Whatever he is, whatever he does, he authentically takes full responsibility for it by not regretting it.

Imagine a parallel universe in which soldier Steve is authentic. How does authentic Steve behave? Authentic Steve recognises that his present situation requires him to play to the full the role of a soldier. This does not mean that he *pretends* to be a soldier. Pretending to be a soldier is what inauthentic Steve does by considering himself to be a civilian disguised as a soldier. In playing at being a soldier to the full, authentic Steve aims at being a soldier to the best of his ability, absorbing himself in his military situation.

He does not believe he is a soldier in the mode of being one, but neither does he disbelieve he is a soldier in the sense of believing that he is really something other than a soldier; something other than his current role. Like Sartre's waiter, he absorbs himself in his performance to the extent that he does not reflect upon the fact that he is performing. He has become his performance and his attitude towards himself involves a suspension of disbelief.

Authenticity is not simply a matter of a person recognising that there are no excuses for his or her actions, he or she must resist by an act of will any desire for excuses. Authentic Steve not only recognises that in his current situation there are no excuses not to play at being a soldier, he does not want there to be any excuses. To be truly authentic, Steve must fully realise his being-in-situation without regret. If authentic Steve does not want to be where he is he will leave without regret and face the consequences of desertion without regret. If he stays, he will assume responsibility for his staying and throw himself into the spirit of things.

Authenticity, as noted, involves a person coming to terms with the fact that she will never become a fixed, substantial entity at one with herself. Contrary to what might be supposed, however, authenticity does not involve abandoning the desire for substantiality and foundation.

The desire to be its own foundation belongs to the very structure of human consciousness and so human consciousness cannot abandon this desire. Any attempt to abandon altogether the desire for foundation, for completeness, collapses into a project of nihilism. In seeking to escape the desire for a firm foundation the nihilist aims at being nothing at all, but nonetheless a nothingness that *is* what it is. The nihilist who aims to *be* nothing is as much in bad faith as the person who aims to *be* something.

The authentic person does not aim at substantiality by means of a futile flight from her freedom. Instead, she aims at substantiality by continually founding herself upon the affirmation of her freedom. The affirmation of her freedom is assumed as her basic principle or ultimate value. She seeks to identify herself with her inalienable freedom, rather than flee her inalienable freedom in the vain hope of identifying herself with the unfree objects that surround her.

The project of authenticity is actually more successful at achieving a kind of substantiality than the project of inauthenticity. This is because the project of authenticity reconciles a person to what she really is, an essentially free being, whereas the project of inauthenticity is only ever a flight from what a person really is towards an unachievable identity with objects. In fleeing freedom a person does not establish a foundation, but in assuming her freedom she establishes freedom itself as a foundation. In assuming her freedom she 'becomes' what she is – free – rather than failing to become what she can never be – unfree. The desire for constancy can only be satisfied by embracing freedom because freedom is the only thing about a person that is constant.

It is important to stress that the form of substantiality arrived at through authenticity is not a fixed state of being. It is logically impossible for consciousness to obtain a fixed state of being by any means and all attempts to do so function in bad faith. The substantiality obtained through authenticity is not achieved by consciousness once and for all, it is a substantiality that has to be continually self-perpetuated and re-assumed.

A person cannot simply *be* authentic, she *has to be* authentic. To declare that she is authentic in the manner of a thing, as a table is a table, is to slide once more into bad faith. Authentic being is not a permanent foundation that a person can choose to establish once and for all at a particular time, but rather a precarious foundation that she must continuously maintain by constantly choosing authentic responses to her situation.

Authenticity is not an essence, it is the way a person chooses to respond to her facticity and the way in which she chooses herself in response to her facticity. Authenticity is the continuous task of choosing responses that affirm freedom and responsibility rather than responses that signify a flight from freedom and responsibility. The authentic person takes on the task of continually resisting the slide into bad faith that threatens every human endeavour.

If authenticity involves living without regret, then the following objection regarding the very possibility of authenticity suggests itself. Arguably, authenticity is impossible because it is impossible to live without regret. Regret, it seems, is an unavoidable part of the human condition because anyone with the capacity to imagine alternatives cannot help wishing, at least occasionally, that they had made a different choice.

Responding to this objection existentialists would argue that it does not show authenticity is impossible, simply that it is very difficult to achieve. If a person can come to regret less, as undoubtedly she can by employing various strategies from yoga to the study of existentialism, then she has the potential to master herself completely and regret nothing.

If pressed, existentialists might concede that the task of complete self-mastery and self-overcoming is too difficult to achieve in one lifetime, particularly for people raised in a culture of regret and recrimination. Yet they will still insist that it is an heroic ideal worth striving for because it is always better for a person to try to get real, get a grip and stand firm than it is for her to give up and tell herself she is a victim of circumstance.

It is better, not least, because a person who constantly strives to confront her situation and overcome it, a person who thereby constantly strives to confront and overcome herself, enjoys dignity and self-respect. A cowardly person, on the other hand, who dwells on regret, refusing to confront her situation and her being in that situation, knows only her own weakness, lack of dignity and sense of defeat.

Arguably, authentic existence as a sustained project can be striven for and is worth striving for but it cannot be achieved. It is the holy grail of existentialism; its unobtainable ideal. Sustained authenticity is conceivable as a logical possibility, but no one can actually achieve it. It is like living without making errors of judgement. We know what it would be to live without making errors of judgement, but there will never be a person who makes no errors of judgement. Bad faith threatens every human endeavour. A person would have to be superhuman to always avoid sliding into bad faith. A person slides into bad faith the moment she ceases consciously resisting the world's endless temptations to slide. Bad faith is too convenient and too seductive to be avoided at all times.

To summarise: authentic existence is a project that has to be continually reassumed. A person is only as authentic as her present act. Even if she has been consistently authentic for a week, if she is not authentic right now then she is not authentic. Given the world's endless temptations to bad faith, the difficulties of resisting regret, the fact that habit and other people's expectations shape a person's being as much as her capacity to choose, it is unrealistic to suppose that anyone can sustain authenticity for a significant period of time. At best, it appears a person can be authentic occasionally, which does not amount to achieving authentic existence as a sustained project. Authentic existence – the sustained project – is an unobtainable existentialist ideal. Nevertheless, it is an ideal worth aiming at.

Before ending this chapter it is worth taking a look at Nietzsche's view of authenticity which focuses on the affirmation of life through the refusal to regret a single moment of it. Nietzsche was a nineteenth-century German philosopher who can be accurately described as an existentialist and whose ideas certainly had a huge influence on the existentialist movement as it gathered pace in the twentieth century.

Bad faith, as we've seen, is a choice not to choose. It is *negative freedom*, freedom that denies, checks and represses itself. To exercise freedom negatively is to adopt what Nietzsche calls the *ascetic ideal*. The ascetic ideal values self-repression and self-denial above all else and for their own sake. A person who adopts the ascetic ideal does not, for example, value celibacy for the sexual health and peace of mind it brings, but only for the self-denial it involves.

Opposite to the ascetic ideal is Nietzsche's notion of the *noble ideal*. The noble ideal involves the positive affirmation of freedom. A noble person positively affirms herself as a free being. She does not deny and repress her freedom but enjoys it and is constantly aware of it. She does this by acting decisively, overcoming difficulties, taking responsibility, choosing her own values and refusing to regret. For Nietzsche, positive freedom is expansive, sometimes even reckless and violent. It triumphs in its own strength as a positive *will to power*.

Will to power, a key idea in Nietzsche's philosophy, can be either positive or negative. Positive will to power is power as it is commonly understood: power that is expansive, even explosive. It's opposite, however, is still will to power. A being that refuses to expand still has will to power. Soldiers making an orderly retreat refuse expansion but this does not mean they have lost their will to power. Likewise, a person who conserves her strength behind a barricade exercises will to power in inviting her enemy to spend her strength attacking that barricade.

For Nietzsche, a person cannot not be a will to power, just as, according to Sartre and de Beauvoir, a person cannot not be free. Whereas Nietzsche has the concepts of positive and negative will to power, Sartre and de Beauvoir have the concepts of the positive freedom of the responsible, authentic person and the negative freedom of the inauthentic person who acts in bad faith choosing not to choose.

For Sartre and de Beauvoir, freedom can come to value itself as the source of all values. This positive freedom involves the same principles as Nietzsche's noble ideal. It is a positive will to power. A person does not achieve a radical conversion to authenticity by rejecting and divorcing her former self through the exercise of bad faith, but by overcoming her former self, her former values, to become the creator of her own values. As the creator of her own values she creates herself; she is the artist or author of her own life.

Whatever a negative person or a person in bad faith identifies as a lamentable experience to be forgotten or denied, the artist or author of her own life, whose aim is to positively affirm her entire life, will identify as a learning experience that helped to make her stronger and wiser. She regrets nothing because every experience has contributed to making her what she is. In Nietzsche's view, she will not even regret her evil qualities, or what other people label her evil qualities. As the source of her own values she re-evaluates her evil qualities as her best qualities. Her ability to do this is a true mark of her authenticity. 'The great epochs of our life are the occasions when we gain the courage to rebaptise our evil qualities as our best qualities' (*Beyond Good and Evil*, 116, p. 97).

In *Crime and Punishment*, a brilliant, existential novel by the Russian author, Fyodor Dostoevsky, the central character Raskolnikov, in an attempt to escape his poverty, kills a mean old pawnbroker and her sister with an axe. After committing double-murder, Raskolnikov tells himself he must strive to be like Napoleon, a man who has the strength of character to justify his crimes to himself. Unfortunately, unlike Napoleon, Raskolnikov lacks the audacity to shoulder his dirty deed and genuinely not care about it. In Nietzsche's words, he lacks the courage, 'To redeem the past and to transform every "It was" into an "I wanted it thus!"' (*Thus Spoke Zarathustra*, p. 161).

As Raskolnikov's ego is not sufficient to swallow the enormity of his crime, his only means of escaping his guilt is to lapse into an attitude of bad faith whereby he disowns himself by disowning his past. This is not to say that to be authentic a person must commit murder without giving a damn about it, but rather that to be authentic a person must take responsibility for all her actions whatever they are rather than try to disown them through bad faith and confession and the belief that she has been 'born again'.

To disown the past in bad faith and to redefine the past by assuming responsibility for it are radically different responses. If the aspiring convert to authenticity is to overcome bad faith she must take responsibility for the whole of her past without regret. A person who regrets wishes her past were different, she wishes she were not the free being she is and has been. A person who regrets fails to affirm the whole of her freedom and hence the whole of her life as the creation of her freedom. Nietzsche holds that the highest affirmation of life is the desire for *eternal recurrence*. For a person to truly affirm her freedom and her life as the creation of her freedom she must embrace the possibility of living it all over again in every detail an infinite number of times. Nietzsche writes:

> The question in each and every thing, 'Do you desire this once more and innumerable times more?' would lie upon your actions as the greatest weight. Or how well disposed would you have to become to yourself and to life *to crave nothing more fervently* than this ultimate eternal confirmation and seal? (*The Gay Science*, 341, p. 274)

Nietzsche's uncompromising thought is that if you don't want to live your life over again then you're not living it right! Almost nobody wants to die. Most of us love life, or at least crave the opportunity to go on perfecting it in whatever future remains to us. But how many of us would actually want to relive a significant proportion of what we've had of our life so far – all that boredom, disappointment, insult, pain and fear? Realistically, could anyone ever become so well disposed towards her life as to crave every detail of it innumerable times?

In professing to love life is it that we love only our future and what we dream of becoming in our future? Does anyone actually love all or even most of their past, rather than just the good times they care to remember? And do you ever meet anyone who is honestly entirely happy with their present situation? And if everyone is unhappy with their present situation *continually* then ...? If nothing else, the idea of eternal recurrence is rich food for thought that raises a lot of important personal and moral questions.

From a metaphysical point of view eternal recurrence is problematic. If eternal recurrence is true, this life must be identical to the infinity of lives you have lived and will live. You can't change anything. And if you can't change anything, you can't be free. That Nietzsche actually believes we live our lives over again an infinite number of times is debatable. Arguably, what matters to him is not whether or not eternal recurrence is the case, but the moral acid test that the very idea of it provides.

So, Nietzsche's answer to the perennial moral question, 'How should I live?', is: aspire to live in such a way that you want each and every moment of your life to recur eternally. Nietzsche calls this his *formula for greatness*. 'My formula for greatness for a human being is *amor fati* [love fate]: that one wants nothing to be other than it is, not in the future, not in the past, not in all eternity' (*Ecce Homo: How one Becomes What One Is*, p. 68). In rejecting and discarding his past like an old overcoat, Raskolnikov fails to adopt Nietzsche's formula for greatness. It almost goes without saying that to become a true existentialist, to achieve authentic existence, you have to embrace Nietzsche's formula for greatness.

Another German existentialist philosopher who was born only a few decades after Nietzsche is Martin Heidegger. Heidegger also has a lot to say about authenticity, but as he focuses on what he calls, *authentic-being-towards-death*, we will postpone exploring his views on authenticity until the final chapter; until the death.

11 Children and Childhood

There is always one moment in childhood when the door opens and lets the future in. (Graham Greene, *The Power and the Glory*, p. 6)

Existentialists are not the type of people to send a card saying, 'Congratulations on the birth of your baby', but then, they are not the type of people to send congratulations and greetings cards full stop.

The polite, reflex reaction of most people when told that someone they know personally is having a baby is to offer congratulations. But how many people really feel that congratulations are in order? Why congratulate a person who is about to sink into a self-inflicted mire of domestic drudgery stinking of vomit and shit? Rather selfishly perhaps, the first thought of many people when they discover a friend is having a baby is, 'Well, that's the end of them as a friend in any practical sense, at least for a number of years.'

Parenthood will almost inevitably disengage them from their broader social group as visits to Mothercare and Legoland take precedence over climbing holidays and weekend raves. They will become invariably busy, tired and distracted. None of their peers will be particularly keen to visit them in their den of diapers, not only because of the smell, but because adult indulgences and uninterrupted grown-up conversation will have been replaced by watching the babe throw-up on its comfort-blanket. 'If you're happy with a nappy then you're in for fun' (Wham!, 'Young Guns').

This is a cynical view no doubt, but certainly one that existentialists would tend to sympathise with. Generally, the existentialists' view of birth is that it is an extremely unfortunate occurrence, both for the parents and for the newborn itself. It is no mere coincidence that none of the great existentialists, as far as I know, had children. Kierkegaard, for example, deliberately gave up his plans for a family when he broke off his engagement to Regine Olsen in 1841 to devote himself to philosophy. Sartre and de Beauvoir were lovers but they made sure no children came of it. De Beauvoir writes:

> I had no dreams urging me to embrace maternity; and to look at the problem another way, maternity itself seemed incompatible with the way of life upon which I was embarking. I knew that in order to become a writer I needed a great measure of time and freedom. (*The Prime of Life*, p. 78)

Admittedly, Sartre had an adopted daughter called Arlette, but she was well out of nappies when he adopted her. In fact, he first met her when she visited his Paris apartment to discuss *Being and Nothingness* for her philosophy dissertation. The perfect child for an existentialist would be born potty trained, addicted to cigarettes and able to discuss the finer points of phenomenological ontology.

Sartre even wrote a novel, *The Age of Reason*, in which the central character, a professor of philosophy called Mathieu Delarue, strives to obtain sufficient funds to have his child aborted before its birth destroys his profligate lifestyle free from bourgeois expectations and constraints.

Nowhere in *The Age of Reason* are children spoken of with any positive regard. The foetus that Mathieu and his partner, Marcelle, have inadvertently conceived is variously described as a tumour, a pustule, a blister, 'a little, vitreous tide within her ... opening out among all the muck inside her belly' (*The Age of Reason*, p. 20). Such are Sartre's thoughts, or at least those of his alter ego, Mathieu.

When Mathieu meets a friend's little boy, far from being moved by the joys of an expectant father, he thinks:

> Pablo's expression was not yet human, and yet it was already more than
> alive: the little creature had not long emerged from a womb, as indeed
> was plain: there he was, hesitant, minute, still displaying the unwholesome
> sheen of vomit: but behind the flickering humours that filled his eye-sockets,
> lurked a greedy little consciousness ... in a pink room, within a female body,
> there was a blister, growing slowly larger. (*The Age of Reason*, pp. 43–44)

Existentialists tend to hold that it is an act of profound bad faith to
have children. To have children is to choose to be determined by the
domestic circumstances child rearing demands rather than a choice to
affirm one's own freedom and creativity. 'Literature, I thought, was a
way of justifying the world by fashioning it anew in the pure context of
imagination ... Childbearing, on the other hand, seemed no more than
a purposeless and unjustifiable increase in the world's population' (*The
Prime of Life*, p. 78). Having a baby threatens, perhaps more than any
other single act, to drive people down into domesticated dullness and
bad faith, down into an insipid and weak minded state where they
hope to evade responsibility for themselves and their destiny by bur-
dening themselves with the responsibility of a child and *its* destiny.

This seems an absurd view given that reproducing is so widespread
and necessary, so natural, but there appears to be some truth in it
when the motives for having children of at least some people are scru-
tinised. That mankind, including existentialists, would soon become
extinct if nobody reproduced, does not mean that having children is
never an act of bad faith. Certainly, some people have children in order
to live for others rather than for themselves, in order to give themselves
a ready-made destiny, in order to avoid the effort required to pursue
their own *genuine* creativity and so on.

Children can be a convenient, guilt free means by which people give
up on themselves. All that can be expected of people with children,
burdened as they are, is that they raise their children well, and often
the self-thwarted ambitions of parents who have chosen to live
vicariously are made to be the responsibility of their offspring. The

anthropologist and sorcerer's apprentice, Carlos Castaneda, says, 'When one has a child that child takes the edge off our spirit' (*The Second Ring of Power*, p. 117). An edge that, in the existentialists' view, many people who have children are quite happy to have taken from them.

In the existentialists' view, if having a baby is a misfortune then being born is a disaster. The average doting, deluded parent may feel that their offspring is a gift from heaven and a necessary being, but the existentialists know that each fleshy, squawking package of desire and dissatisfaction that is born into this cruel world is utterly *superfluous*. It makes no difference that the baby is wanted, that it was planned for, it is nonetheless a cosmic accident, the ultimately absurd and pointless continuation of an absurd and pointless species.

If the existentialists had their way, every baby would be born to the sound of 'Riders on the Storm' by The Doors: 'Into this house we're born, into this world we're thrown, like a dog without a bone, an actor out alone.' This would serve to emphasise that the baby has no *raison d'être*; that the only meaning and purpose it can ever hope to have is the relative meaning and purpose it chooses to give itself as it grows up.

Sartre claims to have recognised the contingency and superfluity of his existence from an early age. His doting family treated the infant Sartre as a necessity, as a being that was meant to be. Sartre, however, precocious youth that he was, saw himself as travelling on a train without a ticket; travelling through life without justification for his absurd existence, troubled by a ticket-inspector that was also himself. 'Stowaway traveller, I had fallen asleep on the seat and the ticket-inspector was shaking me. "Your ticket!" I was forced to admit that I had not got one' (*Words*, p. 70).

We appear on life's train, a train bound for nowhere, ticketless passengers born of equally ticketless passengers, all of us utterly *abandoned* – at least according to atheistic existentialists like Heidegger, Camus, Sartre, de Beauvoir and Beckett. This is not to say we have been abandoned in the sense of 'left behind' or 'neglected' by someone or something. For the philosophers named, there is nothing 'out there' that could have abandoned us in this way. Rather, we are all abandoned because there is no God to give human life purpose or moral direction. We have always been alone and will always be alone in an ultimately meaningless universe. Even if there is intelligent life on other planets, it is equally abandoned and alone in the sense of inhabiting a godless, meaningless universe.

The atheistic existentialists' adoption of the notion of abandonment is the clearest possible expression of their atheism, their view that humankind is a cosmic accident and not the product of some higher design on the part of God or gods. As humans are uncreated – the process of reproduction that works through parents is not *creation* on their part – the idea or essence of each person does not precede his or her existence. People exist first – accidentally, unnecessarily, superfluously – and must invent their meaning and purpose afterwards.

Ultimately, despite the rather negative tone of this chapter so far, atheistic existentialists do not see abandonment as grounds for pessimism. In their abandonment people are free to create themselves and to become masters of their own destiny. To be free of the will and design of a creator, as one of the inescapable existential truths of human existence, is or should be a source of inspiration rather than despair.

Existentialists tend to be more positive about children, or at least more interested in the pathetic, superfluous little creatures, when viewing them from a *developmental* perspective. Existentialists are most interested in the human condition as suffered and endured by full-blown adult consciousnesses, but in recognising that, as the saying goes, 'The child is the father of the man', they are inevitably drawn to study the child's *psychological* progress.

The starting point for the existentialist interested in child development is invariably the work of the Austrian psychiatrist, Sigmund Freud, the founder of psychoanalysis. Freud was not an existentialist but his controversial ideas became so prominent in the first half of the twentieth century that they had a profound influence on many schools of thought, including existentialism. Although the existentialists admire Freud's radicalism and his efforts to think outside the box on the subject of personal development, they have little respect for many of his conclusions and generally tend to disagree with him, though they do agree with him on certain key points.

They certainly *agree* with Freud that the main features of a person's character are formed in her early years in response to her immediate circumstances and her treatment by others. This, in itself, is no great revelation. Anyone can tell you that Laura is the way she is largely because of her early experiences and the way she was brought up. For example, Laura is claustrophobic because her parents often locked her in her room as a child. But Freud in his way and the existentialists in their way go beyond mere cause and effect explanations that rely simply on knowing, for example, that many people who have claustrophobia were confined as children. They undertake to explore and describe the *psychological mechanisms* whereby early experiences shape personality and influence behaviour.

Freud, famously and controversially, places the emphasis on *sexuality*. Freud argues that young children progress through several stages of psycho-sexual development: the oral stage, the anal stage, the phallic stage and the latency period. During each stage the pleasure-seeking energies of the Id – the subconscious mind and the seat of primitive drives and desires – are focused on the erogenous zone where bodily pleasure is felt most acutely at that time. For example, during the oral stage the child is engrossed with the pleasure she receives from her mouth. According to Freud, excessive frustration or satisfaction at any stage can cause a child to become fixated at that stage. A person fixated at the oral stage displays an oral personality characterised by a constant craving for the oral stimulation provided by food, drink, cigarettes, talking, kissing and so on.

The existentialists appreciate what Freud is getting at with all this psycho-sexual stuff, his insight that intimate, seemingly trivial experiences during childhood have a huge influence on adult personality. But they think that he places far too much emphasis on sexuality and sexual development to the exclusion of other factors. Not least, existentialists think that sexuality is a phenomenon that can be further analysed, explained and reduced. It can be subjected to what they call a *phenomenological reduction*. In their view, Freud mistakenly treats sexuality as irreducible, as something fundamental which cannot be further analysed and reduced which is then used as a basis for explaining everything else. The existentialists' view of sexual desire, their phenomenological reduction of this pseudo-irreducible phenomenon, is explored in Chapter 15.

As a response to Freudian psychoanalysis, Sartre founded existential psychoanalysis, a theory that was developed and applied in a clinical setting by the Scottish psychiatrist, R. D. Laing. Both Sartre and Laing argue that to explain a person in terms of pseudo-irreducible drives and desires, as Freud does, is to reduce her to those drives and desires, and hence to explain her away.

Explained in terms of fundamental drives and desires a person loses her unique individuality. She becomes a 'personality type', an oral or an anal personality type for example, rather than a person shaped both by a set of life circumstances unique to her and by her freely chosen responses to those circumstances. Reflecting on the spread of psycho-analysis in France in the 1920s, de Beauvoir says that she and Sartre 'rejected psychoanalysis as a tool for exploring a normal human being' (*The Prime of Life*, p. 21). She goes on to say:

> Freud's pansexualism struck us as having an element of madness about it, besides offending our puritanical instincts. Above all, the importance it attached to the unconscious, and the rigidity of its mechanistic theories, meant that Freudianism, as we conceived it, was bound to eradicate human free will. (*The Prime of Life*, p. 21)

For the existentialists, while sexuality or the lack of it is clearly a key element in the make-up of any personality, individual character is to be explained not by psycho-sexual fixation but by detailed biography. Only an exhaustive exploration of an individual's personal history, guided by the existentialists' insights into the nature of consciousness, choice, freedom, anxiety, bad faith and so on, will reveal what makes a person tick, what makes them feel, value, act and react as they do.

Laura is claustrophobic because her parents often locked her in her room as a child. Certainly, experience teaches us that many people who were excessively confined as children tend to develop the deeper than average aversion to confined spaces known as claustrophobia. But what of the person who was locked in her room as a child who takes up caving as a hobby or mining as a career, or the person who was never confined as a child but who is profoundly claustrophobic? To understand such diversity of outcomes we need, as the existentialists strongly suggest, to do away with neat psychological labels and one size fits all causal theories and really get to grips with each person as a unique individual.

R. D. Laing would argue that even a person with claustrophobia does not *have* claustrophobia in the way that a person *has* flu, for example. Traditional psychiatry identifies claustrophobia as a general condition that people suffer from as though it were an illness. It is assumed that because claustrophobics tend to exhibit similar symptoms they *have* claustrophobia in much the same way as a person *has* a virus. This approach does not so much explain a claustrophobic person as explain her away by characterising her condition as the product of various impersonal processes. No one *has* claustrophobia. Claustrophobia is not an entity that a claustrophobic possesses in common with other claustrophobics but a product of her own unique choice of herself in response to the peculiarities of her own unique situation.

For the clinical psychologist or professional counsellor the main problem with the existential psychoanalytic method is that it can be extremely time consuming as applied to each individual client, which is perhaps the reason why Freudian psychoanalysis is still far more widely practiced than existential psychoanalysis. It is quicker and easier and therefore more economical to take some ready-made psychological categories and to conduct a formulaic assessment that inevitably pigeon-holes people into those categories. To truly understand what makes a person tick can take years, and certainly there can be no pre-determined time limit placed on the task of fathoming a person out.

To demonstrate in detail the methodology of existential psychoanal-ysis, Sartre wrote several large biographies of French writers: Baude-laire, Genet and Flaubert. Each biography was longer than the last with Sartre's *unfinished* biography of Flaubert, *The Family Idiot*, running to nearly 3000 pages. This work has been described as the most ambi-tious attempt ever made by one human being to understand another, but clearly, if this is what is required to truly understand a person then most people are going to remain more or less a mystery to everyone including themselves.

To be fair, Sartre was out to *totalise* Flaubert, to synthesise the results of an analytic/psychoanalytic investigation of Flaubert's personality with the results of a sociological investigation of Flaubert's economic, politi-cal, historical and cultural context. Sartre even thought that to truly understand Flaubert as a totality, as a unified whole, it was essential to acquire a detailed understanding of nineteenth-century French litera-ture and Flaubert's complex relationship with it.

Sartre went so far with 'The Flaubert', as he nicknamed it, not least because he was also exploring his own personality as a French writer by comparing himself with Flaubert. So, in writing 'The Flaubert', Sartre was in some senses continuing to write his autobiography, continuing to explore why he had chosen writing as his *raison d'être*.

Fortunately, it appears that existential psychoanalysis can yield valu-able insights into a person without the need to go to the extent Sartre did with Flaubert. Only when the subject is a great writer, perhaps, is the analyst required to understand that person's complex relationship with literature. A relationship which may well have begun, as it did with Sartre himself, at a very early age. Sartre tells us in yet another of his biographies of French writers – his own – how he devoured his grandfather's library before the age of ten.

At the heart of existential psychoanalysis is the analyst's search for a person's unique *fundamental choice* of herself and the *fundamental project* that stems from that fundamental choice. A unique fundamental choice of self is, in the existentialists' view, what shapes each and every person and makes them tick. For the existentialists, fundamental choice replaces the Freudian notion of personality type.

To understand the meaning of *fundamental choice* it is necessary to recall the existentialists' claim that consciousness is constituted as a lack of being that has the fundamental project of overcoming that lack. As a lack of being, consciousness aims to be being. It aims to be complete; a godlike being in which existence and essence are one. Existentialists are fond of saying that to be God is the fundamental project of human reality. As Sartre says, 'To be man means to reach towards being God. Or if you prefer, man fundamentally is the desire to be God' (*Being and Nothingness*, p. 587).

In the everyday, concrete situation of an individual person the general project of desiring to be God, of desiring to be totally fulfilled, is expressed in the form of a desire to be united with a particular way of being that is perceived to be presently lacking. The project of seeking unity with a particular way of being that a person perceives to be presently lacking is the fundamental project of that person.

Her particular fundamental project is established via an original or fundamental choice whereby she chooses herself as a particular kind of lack. In choosing herself as a particular kind of lack she constantly chooses to project herself towards the ends that would overcome that lack. Indeed, her personality is comprised of the host of behaviours and attitudes that she employs in her constant effort to overcome the particular lack that she has chosen to be.

To take a simple example, a person may fundamentally choose herself as lacking equal status with others, as essentially inferior, and as a result spend the rest of her life striving to overcome that lack. She may project an air of superiority and her achievements may far outstrip those of her peers, but it will all be rooted in that fundamental choice of herself as inferior which she constantly affirms by the very fact that she is constantly motivated to refute it.

Alternatively, a person may project an air of superiority and strive to achieve more than her peers because she has indeed chosen herself as superior. She will continue to lack superiority as a possession – there is nothing that she is or can be in the manner of simply *being* it and it is impossible for her to be a superior-*thing* – but she may nonetheless spend her entire life affirming that fundamental choice of herself as superior which she once adopted as a reaction to her essential nothingness and indeterminacy.

It is even possible for a person to project an air of inferiority and underachieve precisely because she has chosen herself as superior, but is embarrassed and ashamed of that fundamental choice of herself as superior. Only a detailed analysis of personal history can hope to reveal the truth.

A fundamental choice is not the product of antecedent tendencies. Rather, it is the basis of all consequent ones. As an aspect of the dawning of self-consciousness, it is an original choice of self made in response to an event in early life. The event demands that some original choice or other of self be made. Though the event may be trivial in itself, it is, nonetheless, as Sartre says, 'the crucial event of infancy' (*Being and Nothingness*, p. 590). It is crucial because it is here that a person first begins to choose those responses that affirm or deny her view of herself as a certain kind of character.

As a choice of self that establishes grounds for subsequent choosing, the fundamental choice is itself groundless. Though the fundamental choice is groundless, it is nonetheless necessary in that it cannot not be made. Consciousness, as a lack of being, must choose some particular project or other through which it can aim to overcome the lack of being that it is. The fundamental project upon which consciousness embarks depends upon the fundamental choice it makes as to the value and meaning of its own lack of being.

Recall Sartre's childhood view of himself as a stowaway travelling on a train without a ticket. This was how he represented his own indeterminacy and absurd superfluity to himself, his essential lack of being, his nothingness. Realising that he had no ticket, that nobody had or could have given him a ticket, how was he to justify his presence on the train? Well, from the age of seven, Sartre chose writing as his ticket to life and his reason to be. His choice to be a writer was his fundamental choice of himself, a choice that influenced all his subsequent choices and so shaped his entire life and personality.

> I was born from writing: before that, there was only a reflection in a mirror. From my first novel, I knew that a child had entered the palace of mirrors. By writing, I existed, I escaped from the grown-ups; but I existed only to write and if I said: me – that meant the me who wrote. (*Words*, p. 97)

Sartre claims in *Words* that it was his desire for heroic immortality as a writer, set alongside his early dismissal of Christian notions of salvation and the afterlife, that motivated him rather than any particular gift or genius. He is fond of arguing that genius is as genius does. 'The genius of Proust is the totality of the works of Proust; the genius of Racine is the series of his tragedies, outside of which there is nothing' (*Existentialism and Humanism*, pp. 41–42). Sartre deliberately set out from childhood to create himself as a 'genius' through sustained hard work and unflinching self-belief.

Constantly making himself a writer through the act of writing enabled Sartre to maintain an illusion of substance and purpose that effectively kept at bay those disturbing childhood feelings of pointlessness and superfluity. He maintained this grand illusion so well by his efforts, believed so strongly in his vocation, in his capacity to achieve his destiny, that as a young man he was, unlike his friends, untroubled by fears of an untimely death. 'I had forearmed myself against accidental death, that was all; the Holy Ghost had commissioned a long-term work from me, so he had to give me time to complete it' (*Words*, pp. 123–124).

Towards the end of *Words* the ageing writer finally writes himself out of the grand illusion that has sustained him since childhood. He finally confronts what he has always known, what he has spent the greater part of his life striving to deny, that writing or any other activity cannot remove his superfluity and make him a necessary being at one with himself. Like everyone else he remains a ticketless traveller on a journey to nowhere. 'I have become once again the traveller without a ticket that I was at seven' (*Words*, p. 157). Despite his monumental efforts he remains contingent and mortal, his immortal status as a writer existing only for future generations of equally contingent mortals.

The fundamental choice is the original and most fundamental attempt on the part of consciousness to escape the utter contingency and superfluity of its being. By choosing itself as a particular kind of lack it hopes to make sense of its being by overcoming that lack; as though in a final act of complete overcoming it could establish an ultimate *raison d'être* for its otherwise contingent being. But of course, there can be no final act of overcoming whereby consciousness establishes itself as a determinate, necessary being once and for all.

Though consciousness constantly aims to overcome the lack that it is, it can never do so. Only death can annihilate the lack that a person is. Only by ceasing to exist at all can a person finally cease to exist as a being that constantly lacks identity with herself. Death transforms her life into a fixed entity, not for her but for other people, although even then what she was is open to endless interpretation.

So, a person is the product of her choices. The core of her personality is not a fixed nature or essence but her fundamental childhood choice of herself. The actions that a person chooses in response to her fundamental choice comprise her fundamental project. Often a life is defined by a single fundamental project based on a single fundamental choice. However, existentialists hold that it is possible for a person to undergo a *radical conversion* in which she establishes a new fundamental choice of herself. After all, at the risk of stating the obvious, fundamental choice is a *choice*, an expression of freedom that endures only because it is chosen. As a choice it is forever susceptible to freedom, to conversion, to being radically overthrown by a new fundamental choice.

The type of radical conversion that existentialists are most interested in is the radical conversion from bad faith to authenticity, and by 'radical conversion' they generally mean 'radical conversion to authenticity', although they allow that a radical conversion in the opposite direction is also possible.

Radical conversion to authenticity involves a person abandoning a fundamental project in which she strives in her own particular way to deny that she is free, in favour of a new fundamental project in which she affirms her freedom and takes full responsibility for herself and her being-in-situation.

According to Sartre, the French writer, Gustave Flaubert, underwent a radical conversion in his twenties. This was yet another reason why Sartre thought Flaubert worthy of that vast biography, *The Family Idiot*, a work that dominated the last few years of Sartre's working life and helped to send him blind.

According to Sartre, Gustave's mother wanted a daughter, a female companion to compensate for her lonely childhood. Her husband was no companion, he had lost interest in her and was having affairs. Furthermore, baby Gustave was not expected to survive as the two siblings immediately preceding him had died. As a result, the disappointing, futureless child received skilful care, the aim of which was to pacify him, but very little real maternal affection. Sartre identifies Flaubert's passivity as his *first* fundamental choice of himself. He was not encouraged to respond, to feel that he had a purpose, to feel that he could be something more than an object his mother was obliged to care for.

Gustave faired no better with his father, whose attentions and hopes were directed towards Gustave's older brother, Achille, who eventually became a successful doctor like his father. Pacified, overlooked as a person, Gustave's intellectual development was slow. He was unable to read at the age of seven. His family further reinforced the low self-esteem at the heart of his ennui by viewing him as an idiot.

Gustave was eventually taught to read by the local priest. Though still passive in his general demeanour and given to meditative stupors that made him appear a simpleton, Gustave took possession of his new found ability and by the age of nine was writing stories. Gustave's father decided, however, that Gustave would be a lawyer. Passive as ever, Gustave followed this plan, all the while developing a nervous disorder.

The defining moment of Gustave's life occurred in 1844 when he suffered a nervous crisis, possibly an epileptic fit. Incapacitated by this crisis he was unable to pursue the legal career his father had chosen for him. Gustave's crisis, arguably self-induced, allowed him to finally free himself from his father's domination and become a writer. The invalid, being no good for anything better, was left to write. The idiot was at last free to transform himself into a genius.

For Sartre, Flaubert's nervous crisis was in reality a radical conversion to authenticity, an act of self-assertion in which he finally dispensed with his passivity, his choice not to choose, his bad faith. Through an act that had the outward appearance of a mental collapse, but was, in fact, a positive affirmation of freedom, he finally abandoned his fundamental choice to exist *passively* for other people in favour of a new fundamental choice to exist *actively* for himself.

12 Other People

The eyes of others our prisons; their thoughts our cages. (Virginia Woolf, *Monday or Tuesday*, p. 22)

I am 'alone' in my study right now, looking out of the window for the inspiration to start this chapter. A cocky, bearded, red-faced guy in a tweed flat cap struts down the street and looks up at me looking out of the window. So I look down at him looking up at me and we form prejudiced opinions about each other and feel slightly annoyed that we are being looked at. We are always being looked at, and even when we are not we often feel we are, so pervasive is the existence of other people in our lives.

Existentialists recognise that the existence of other people is one of the inescapable truths of the human condition. In fact, they argue that the existence of others is so fundamental to our own existence that an important part of what we are exists for others, exists in relation to others, exists to be shaped by others and so on. They call this our *being-for-others*.

Even the recluse or hermit who takes to living in the middle of nowhere to get away from everyone still inhabits a world where others exist. She may occasionally have to come into contact with others to obtain the basic supplies she needs to live, and even if she has become totally self-sufficient it was not always so. Doubtless her so-called self-sufficiency will be based on having once collected tools and materials manufactured by others without which she could not survive. Robinson Crusoe survived alone on his island for years but only because he was able to salvage from the wreck of his ship many essentials that other people had produced, from knives, hatchets, guns and ammunition to rope, nails, barrels and biscuits.

Every so-called self-sufficient adult was once a totally dependent child, and, to state the obvious, our very entry into the world involves an intimate biological relationship with another person. Even when we are alone other people tend to be in our thoughts. We miss them and think about what we would say to them if they were present, or we regret what we said to them or they said to us last time we spoke and feel embarrassed or angry about it.

As we have seen, each person is a being-for-itself; a unique, embodied point of view on the world with her own intentions, goals and values. Each person is a free transcendence striving against the facticity of the world to fulfil herself through her choices and actions. But each person, each transcendence, is also an object for other people; a being at the mercy of the look, the intentions, the evaluations, the transcendence *of other people*.

In simply being conscious of me, other people force me to be what I am for them. I may revel in their opinion of me if it is positive, even if I know it to be false. If it is a negative opinion, as it often is, I am likely to want to alter it or to convince myself that its holder is of no account. I may even seek to escape their opinion altogether by creating myself anew so that it is no longer an opinion that applies to me. All these means aim essentially at the reassertion of my own free transcendence over the free transcendence of other people. Let's look at all this more closely.

Not every feature of our conscious existence can be accounted for simply in terms of being-for-itself. Certain key features of our conscious existence are essentially *Other related*; they belong to our being-for-others. One of the most familiar Other related feature of ourselves, one which we experience or feel in danger of experiencing every day of our lives, one which few people could honestly claim never to have experienced, is *embarrassment*.

Embarrassment is *for* consciousness, and a person is embarrassed in so far as she is conscious of being embarrassed. However, although embarrassment very much characterises the self of the person suffering it, a person does not realise embarrassment for herself and by herself. Embarrassment requires a direct apprehension of another person (the Other) as a conscious being who sees her and judges her. Embarrassment requires self-reflection. It is, after all, an uncomfortably acute form of self-consciousness. Primarily, however, it is embarrassment *before somebody*.

A person can, of course, experience embarrassment when alone, but such private embarrassment always refers back to others. A person can become embarrassed by her *recollection* of an encounter with another, even if she did not think to be embarrassed at the time. A person can become embarrassed wondering if perhaps she was seen doing an improper thing. A person can become embarrassed simply by imagining how awful it would be to be caught *in flagrante delicto*. To understand what is involved in being seen and judged, as an experience that is not merely comprehended but lived and suffered, is to understand the meaning and significance of being-for-others.

Human beings are objects. They have bodies, objects that are externally related to other objects and which are affected by the same physical determinants that affect all objects. However, although human beings are objects and the Other is a human being, it is not as an object that the Other is originally revealed to me as Other. So how is the Other revealed to me?

It is useful to begin with an example in which the Other does not encounter me. An example in which I simply see another person who does not see me. This example outlines certain structures that help elucidate the case we are most interested in, the case of being encountered by the Other. I see a woman on an otherwise empty beach. Immediately, my awareness of the woman's presence on the beach affects my situation. The woman's appearance constitutes the start of the disintegration of the world from my own point of view. Suddenly, the situation, which was mine to evaluate as I wished, contains a new source of values which are not mine and which escape me. I am decentralised by the appearance of the Other.

The reorientation of the world towards the woman, the fact that meanings unknown to me flow in her direction, constitutes her as a drain hole down which my own world flows. The term 'drain hole' in this context is borrowed from Sartre and is perhaps his least flattering way of describing the Other. 'Rather it appears that the world has a kind of drain hole in the middle of its being and that it is perpetually flowing off through this hole' (*Being and Nothingness*, p. 279).

It is because the Other is this drain hole that a person enjoying solitude in the wilds will feel annoyed when she sees another person, even if that other person does not see her. The very appearance of another person prevents her from playing God. She ceases to be the centre and sole judge of all she surveys because a source of re-evaluation has appeared on the scene to steal the world away from her and with it her glorious, godlike supremacy. Have you ever felt that a tranquil woodland path with one stranger walking towards you, or walking behind you, or even walking ahead of you and oblivious of you, was more crowded than Piccadilly Circus?

So far, the woman on 'my' beach is still only a special kind of object. Although she is a drain hole in my world and a threat to the centralisation I bring about, she remains an object in my world. However, that I recognise her as a threat to my centralisation suggests that there are occasions when this threat is realised; occasions when the Other effects a radical reorientation of my being.

The existentialists insist that the mere gaze of the Other fixes me as an object in the world of the Other. As an object for the Other I am a *transcendence-transcended* by the transcendence of the Other. I cease to exist primarily as a free subject for myself and exist instead primarily as an un-free object for others. As with many aspects of existentialist theory, this radical reorientation is best explained with a concrete example to which we can all relate.

CCTV and the internet can now make petty, immoral acts, that in the past people tended to get away with, into world-wide media sensations. So, beware how you conduct yourself on all occasions, there is a good chance the Big Brother Other is watching you. The example I'm thinking of is that of an English woman who in 2010 was caught on CCTV throwing a friendly young cat called Lola into a wheelie bin. The footage has been viewed millions of times on websites such as You-Tube and will be viewed millions of times more in the future. Cruelty to cats is a terrible thing but the hatred and censure the woman has endured and will continue to endure is out of proportion to her crime, precisely because she is destined to commit her crime *ad infinitum* and to be condemned *ad infinitum*.

People who have done worse things to animals are still walking about with their heads held high, either because the cruelty they displayed was more socially acceptable, like fox hunting or dog fighting, or because it was not caught on CCTV. I knew of someone who threw a live hamster onto a fire, but as this was never filmed they probably go about today thinking of themselves as a good person.

The woman claims that to this day she has no idea why she put the cat in the wheelie bin, and my purpose here is not to psychoanalyse her motives. Perhaps she had a grudge against the owners or was having a bad morning. Perhaps she did it simply because she was free to do so and wanted to assert that freedom. What concerns us here is not her motives but the radical reorientation of her being that occurred the instant she knew she was exposed.

During her crime and for a blissfully ignorant period afterwards she remained a free transcendence. Certainly, during her crime, as a subject absorbed in what she was doing, she did not judge herself. She knew in a general sense that what she was doing was wrong, that others would consider it so, but at the time of acting she did not pass this judgement of wrongness upon herself because she was too wrapped up in the thrill of the moment to really see herself from an external point of view.

She did not know her actions, she was them. She freely transcended the meaning of her act even as she performed it and did not have to define herself as petty and spiteful. Later on, if she reflected on her act, she perhaps avoided branding herself as petty and spiteful by telling herself that her act was simply an aberration or a self-dare, a meaningless distraction with no bearing on her character or morals. Perhaps she told herself that a person's present self cannot be held responsible for past conduct. Indulging in bad faith she might have reasoned that she had already ceased to be the person she was.

Suddenly, however, the footage is on the news or the police are at the door. What ghastly self-realisation and profound mortification she must have suffered in that first moment, the echoes of which will never die away for her. How she must have wished that her crime was less pathetic and ridiculous, something less embarrassing with more kudos, like theft or murder.

What she did, what she is, is now revealed to the Other and thereby very painfully to herself. All at once, her act, which for her had little or no meaning, has escaped her and acquired vast meaning for the Other. It now belongs to the Other for whom she has become an object of perpetual contempt. Her freedom is enslaved by the freedom of the Other. In catching her in the act the Other has caught her freedom, transcended her transcendence, and is at liberty to judge her and inflict meanings upon her: mean, mad, monstrous, misguided, a crusader against the feline menace.

In the mode of being-for-itself the self is precisely not an object. As a negation of being it is founded upon a being that it is not. It is not in the world as objects are but as a transcendence. Heidegger refers to this way of being as *being-in-the-world*. Being-in-the-world refers to a person's being for herself as a being that constantly projects herself beyond the world, beyond the present, towards her possibilities. For herself, a person is not a thing alongside other things. She is not *in* being. Rather, she is that which freely transcends being towards the future. Being-in-the-world refers to the transcendent aspect of her being.

The self, however, has another mode of being that Heidegger refers to as *being-in-the-midst-of-the-world*. Being-in-the-midst-of-the-world refers to a person's presence in the world as an object amongst other objects. Here, as in the case of the cat woman, her free transcendence is transcended by the Other and she becomes a thing alongside other things. She is still her possibilities, but these possibilities are now a given fact for the Other. They belong also to the Other and are subject to the Other's judgement. This mode of being corresponds to a person's being-for-others and is realised when she experiences herself as seen by the Other or when she regards herself from the point of view of the Other.

When a person experiences herself as seen by the Other she immediately ceases to be a transcendent subject, a pure point of view upon the world, and becomes instead an object in the midst of the world seen from the point of view of the Other. Importantly, to experience herself as an object for the Other is to experience the Other as a subject. It is this direct and unmediated experience of herself as an object for the Other's subjectivity that reveals the Other to her as Other.

She experiences the Other through the immediate negation of her own transcendent subjectivity by the transcendent subjectivity of the Other. To experience the Other is for a person to exist her own being as a transcendence-transcended. 'The other as a look is only that – my transcendence transcended' (*Being and Nothingness*, p. 287).

A person's being-for-others is very much a being that she is, but she is it over there, for the Other, in so far as the Other is free to interpret and evaluate her actions at will. A person's being-for-others constitutes a whole range of (her) possibilities, but they are alienated possibilities. They are not possibilities that she maintains and controls through her own transcendence, but possibilities fixed by the transcendence of the Other.

Embarrassment is one way in which being-for-others is revealed existentially, but alongside embarrassment can be listed such related phenomena as shame, guilt and paranoia. Being-for-others, however, is not limited to these unpleasant states of being. Being-for-others also accounts for pleasant states such as feeling proud, flattered or indulged. Pleasure is gained here precisely because a person makes herself an object for the Other.

In making herself an object for the Other she enjoys relinquishing responsibility for her free transcendence; a responsibility that, as we have seen, may well be a source of anxiety. She may also take pleasure in reflecting on the pleasing object that she is for the Other. Interestingly, existentialists argue that the basis of the masochist's pleasure is that he or she is a sexualised *object* for the Other. Being-for-other is, not surprisingly, an integral aspect of sexual relationships and sexual desire. Sexual desire is explored in Chapter 15.

It is important to note that the look of the Other does not permanently render a person an object for the Other. It is not the case that when the Other has transcended her transcendence she remains a transcendence permanently transcended. A person can also become Other for the Other by recovering her transcendence, thereby reducing the Other to an object. This is certainly the case in genuine interpersonal relationships where a person will find the opportunity to recover her transcendence. Indeed, if the Other is at all well disposed towards her this recovery will be positively encouraged.

It appears, however, that there are some relationships where a recovery of subjectivity appears to be impossible. In the relationship between a person and a CCTV camera, for example, a stable situation exists in which there is no possibility of returning the look the camera gives. The transcendence of a person's transcendence by a camera cannot be reversed; a person cannot become Other for the Other and so regain her transcendence. It is not possible to outstare a camera. And when the power of the internet to broadcast CCTV images *ad nauseam* humiliates a person *ad nauseam* the transcendence is even more of an irreversible one-way street. It is an utter, ceaseless, irrecoverable objectification.

Technology aside, if we can put it aside, existentialists tend to characterise ordinary interpersonal relations as a ceaseless, irresolvable power struggle. Schopenhauer, Nietzsche and Sartre, for example, are certainly of the opinion that *conflict* is the essence of all human relationships. Conflict may involve a struggle to dominate the transcendence of the Other and render it a transcendence-transcended. This is the most familiar form of power struggle. Alternatively, for masochists, it will involve conflict over who gets to be dominated, but more of that in Chapter 15.

Sartre's vision of hell, as depicted in his most famous play, *In Camera* (also called *Behind Closed Doors* or *No Exit*), is simply three people trapped forever in a drawing room endlessly seeking to justify themselves and get the better of each other. The play progresses through mounting conflict towards Sartre's damning conclusion, possibly the most famous lines he ever wrote, 'There's no need for red-hot pokers. Hell is other people!' (*In Camera*, p. 223).

The triangle of love and hate that the three characters in the play form is loosely based on the emotionally charged ménage à trois involving Sartre, de Beauvoir and Russian born Olga Kosakiewicz. Olga was a beautiful, intelligent, proud and capricious young woman who had been a student of Simone de Beauvoir's in Rouen in the early 1930s. Sartre and de Beauvoir decided early on that their unique personal and intellectual relationship constituted a 'necessary love' that could tolerate and even benefit from the 'contingent love' of their various affairs. The passions that Olga stirred in both of them seriously challenged this arrangement. The necessary love between Sartre and de Beauvoir was threatened above all by Sartre's intense infatuation with Olga and his jealous, thwarted desire to possess her.

From 1935 to 1937, as Sartre tried everything in his power to win Olga, her refusal either to accept or reject him drove him to near madness and despair. Sartre later claimed he never knew jealousy except where Olga was concerned and undoubtedly his affair with her was a life-defining episode that haunted his writing for many years.

Several of Sartre's female characters have some of Olga's personality traits. The ménage à trois at the centre of de Beauvoir's 1943 novel, *She Came to Stay*, is also based on the ménage à trois involving herself, Sartre and Olga. The most detailed account of the actual affair, an affair so pivotal to the intellectual and emotional development of these two great existentialists, is found in de Beauvoir's autobiography, *The Prime of Life* (pp. 254–263).

Some critics resist the existentialists' claim that the essence of all relationships is conflict, not because they think it is too pessimistic, but simply because they think it is an unjustifiable generalisation. We only have to reflect on the endless conflict that dominates the news – cruelty, violence, exploitation, injustice – to see that the existentialists have a point, nevertheless, most of the time most people actually get along reasonably well.

Even the Sartre, de Beauvoir, Olga triangle, as described biographi-cally rather than caricatured for dramatic purposes, was as much a source of joy to the participants as a source of misery, and there were many happy times when three was not a crowd. To suggest, as the existentialists do, that the look of the Other is always threatening, is to ignore the evidence of certain concrete situations in which the look is clearly not threatening. Turning her critical gaze on Sartre, Marjorie Grene invites us to consider, 'The rare but still indubitable experience of mutual understanding, of the reciprocal look of peers; or the look of mother and infant, where the one protects and the other is protected. In its immediate appearance there seems no internecine warfare here' (*Sartre*, p. 154).

Arguably, the existentialists' insistence on the universality of conflict is motivated too much by personal considerations. The French existen-tialists in particular lived through hugely troubled times. World War I cast a shadow over their childhoods and their progress to intellectual maturity was coloured first by the Spanish Civil War and then by World

War II. It is little wonder that their personal experiences led them to over-emphasise one aspect of human nature.

To be fair to the French existentialists, they did grow to appreciate Heidegger's notion of *mitsein*: 'being-with', 'being-with-others', the phenomenon of 'we'. They came to recognise that their conflict orientated account of being-for-others, in which each person struggles to reduce the Other to a transcendence-transcended, is incomplete as it makes no reference to situations in which a person is in community with the Other rather than in conflict with her.

The question is, how is it possible for there to be a 'we' subject in which a plurality of subjectivities apprehend one another as transcendences-transcending rather than as transcendences-transcended? The answer is that for the 'we' to occur there must be a common action, a collective enterprise or an object of common perception that is the explicit object of consciousness.

For example, a member of an audience absorbed in watching a play is explicitly conscious of the play rather than the audience around her. In being explicitly conscious of the play, however, she is also implicitly or indirectly conscious of being conscious of the play and of being a co-spectator of the play. Being-with can only occur in this implicit, indirect way. It cannot be the explicit object of consciousness. If a spectator makes her fellow spectators the explicit object of her consciousness, rather than the shared experience of the play, she will cease to be a co-spectator with them of the play and they will cease to be her fellow spectators. Her being-with them as part of a 'we' will be lost as they become the object of her consciousness and she transcends their transcendence.

Being-with-others as submergence in an *us*, as submergence in some collective experience or enterprise, is often maintained through conflict with a *them* as opponent or hate object – conflict at the group level. Happily, however, there appear to be some occasions when an *us* does not require a *them* in order to exist. For example, a group may work together on a task with a common goal that is not primarily the goal of beating the competition. Alternatively, a group united together by religion, music, dancing or drugs may achieve a state of reverie or synergy amounting to a collective loss of self.

Interestingly, in her autobiography, *The Prime of Life*, Simone de Beauvoir describes having a revelation, not of her being for herself or her being-for-others, but of her being *just another person*. De Beauvoir, as you might expect, being a true existentialist, prided herself on her independence and self-reliance. In the late 1930s, however, she was taken so seriously ill with pneumonia that she had to place herself entirely in the care of other people in order to survive. She describes the distress and surprise she felt as two male nurses stretchered her from her hotel room. Strangers on the street watched as the nurses loaded her into an ambulance. She was suddenly just anyone. Just one more health statistic. She thought:

> This is really happening, and it's happening to *me* … Anything, it was clear, could happen to me, just as it could to any other person. Now here was a revolution … Sickness, accidents and misfortunes were things that happened only to other people; but in the eyes of those curious bystanders *I* had abruptly become 'other people', and, like all such, I was to all 'other people' just 'another person' myself. (*The Prime of Life*, p. 292)

13 The Body

And nothing *in the visual field* allows you to infer that it is seen by an eye.
(Ludwig Wittgenstein, *Tractatus Logico-Philosophicus*, prop. 5.633)

Although blindingly obvious it is important to state that every person has a body and that the human body is therefore fundamental to the human condition.

The distinction between being-for-itself and being-for-others provides the perfect basis for a philosophical investigation of the body because being-for-itself and being-for-others are the two essential ways in which the body exists, just as they are the two essential ways in which consciousness exists. At the heart of the existentialists' view of the body is the recognition of a radical difference between the way a person's body exists for the person herself and the way it exists for other people.

Whether or not we like to admit it, human beings are objects. The human body is an object amongst other objects that is affected by the same physical conditions that affect all objects. Heidegger, as seen, refers to this as *being-in-the-midst-of-the-world*. This is a person's being considered from the point of view of others. People, however, have another way of being which Heidegger refers to as *being-in-the-world*. In this mode of being, which corresponds to being-for-itself, the body is not an object. Of course, to say that a person's body is not an object for her when she is in the mode of being-in-the-world, when she is transcending the world, is not to say that her body mysteriously ceases to be an object from the point of view of others.

Nevertheless, the claim is that when she is in the mode of being-in-the-world her body is in a certain sense invisible to her, or, at least, that she is oblivious to her body as a thing. Although it happens to be the case that a person can see and touch her own body, it is not essential to her being-in-the-world that she can do so. It is possible for there to be a conscious creature that cannot see or touch its own body, a creature that spends its entire life unaware that it has a body. You cannot, after all, see your eyes without the aid of a mirror, and if your eyes were on long stalks that did not bend back you would be unable to see your body.

Although a person can see her eyes in a mirror, the fact that the eyes in the mirror are the very same eyes that are seeing their reflection cannot be inferred directly from the eyes in the mirror, the eyes in the visual field. To infer that the eyes in the mirror are also the eyes seeing their reflection a person must know certain facts about mirrors and reflection. However, even when a person knows from experience that the eyes in the mirror are the eyes seeing the eyes in the mirror, the eyes in the mirror and the eyes seeing the eyes in the mirror remain *ontologically distinct* – they belong, so to speak, to two different orders of reality.

The eyes in the mirror, though she knows they are nobody's eyes but her own, remain other. They are objects in the visual field. She sees them only as objects. She does not and cannot see the eyes seeing. It would be the same if, strange girl, she had eyes on stalks such that one of her eyes could see the other eye seeing the world. The eye seeing the eye seeing the world would not *see the seeing*. Sartre, imagining that one of his eyes was seeing the other, says:

> I am the *Other* in relation to my eye … I can not 'see the seeing;' that is, I can not apprehend it in the process of revealing an aspect of the world to me. Either it is a thing among other things, or else it is that by which other things are revealed to me. But it can not be both at the same time. (*Being and Nothingness*, p. 328)

However you imagine it – an eye seeing itself in a mirror or one eye somehow seeing the other eye directly – the point is that consciousness is not a ghostly phenomenon magically installed inside the body that can be observed deep within eyes in the form of a seen seeing. Rather, a person's body, as it is for the person herself, is at one with her consciousness, it is wholly psychic, it exists entirely as being-for-itself.

The body is that immediate and inescapable situation which every conscious being must perpetually transcend towards future situations. Consciousness is, however, perpetually re-arrested by the body because the body is the very possibility, the very ground, of the transcendence of consciousness. In other words, consciousness is that which perpetually surpasses the body towards its possibilities without ever being able to render the body finally and completely surpassed.

If consciousness were somehow able to surpass the body once and for all instead of being a perpetual surpassing of it, consciousness would immediately cease to be. This is because the body is the immediate and ever present situation of consciousness. For consciousness, to be and to be situated are one and the same. In existing as a surpassing of the body, consciousness necessarily requires the body in order to realise itself as that which is nothing beyond the surpassing of the body.

This view of the body can be described in temporal terms: consciousness, as a project towards the future, renders the body past (surpassed). The body, however, remains as an immediate past touching upon the present that consciousness always requires in order to launch itself towards the future. Consciousness requires the body as the future requires the past.

What does the fact that consciousness perpetually surpasses the body towards the future fulfilment of its projects imply about the body as an instrument? What, existentialists ask, is the *instrumental status* of a person's body as it is for the person herself? Well, imagine a person absorbed in the task of writing. From the point of view of other people, a person who is writing utilises her hand as an instrument in order to utilise the pen as an instrument. For herself, however, she does not utilise her hand, she utilises the pen in a hand that is herself. Her hand is surpassed towards the project of writing and as such is not an object-hand. Her hand is not acted upon by her consciousness, it is her consciousness acting in the world. 'I am not in relation to my hand in the same utilising attitude as I am in relation to the pen; I *am* my hand … The hand is only the utilisation of the pen' (*Being and Nothingness*, p. 347).

Sartre followed Heidegger in arguing that the human world can be viewed as an infinity of potential systems of instrumentality. For a particular system of instrumentality to emerge from undifferentiated being – for it to become an actual system of instrumentality – there must be an arresting of references to which the entire system refers. That is, any system of instrumentality, in order for it to be a system of instrumentality, must refer back to that for which it is a system of instrumentality.

In the case of the person who is writing, the hand is not an instrument in the system, but that to which an entire system of instrumentality refers. The system of instrumentality emerges by virtue of its orientation towards the hand in action. That is, towards the consciousness in action. The hand in action arrests the system, determines it, orientates it, gives it meaning and so on. At the same time the system gives meaning to the activity of the hand.

What can be said of the hand can also be said of consciousness. A person's consciousness, which from the point of view of another person is amid the instrumentality of the world, is for the person herself the meaning and orientation of the system of instrumentality that she discloses through her purposeful activity.

Just as consciousness surpasses the hand and makes it vanish as an object, so it can surpass the tool the hand is manipulating and make it vanish also. When a person has learnt to use a tool skilfully the tool is forgotten while in use; it is surpassed towards the task. It exists in the mode of what Heidegger refers to as *ready-to-hand*. The tool becomes an extension of the body as the person acts towards her future goals. The body, so to speak, extends through the tool she utilises. It is there at the end of the screwdriver that turns the screw or even at the end of the turning screw as it taps into the wall. When a person pokes dirt with a stick in order to discover if it is soft or hard she feels the texture of the dirt there at the end of the stick, at which moment she does not feel the stick in her hand.

Tools tend only to assert their independence from a person and remind her of their existence when they fail, or when she fails to manipulate them correctly. That is, when they suddenly cease to be an instrument for her and instead present themselves as an obstacle. Here they present themselves in the manner of what Heidegger refers to as *present-at-hand*.

A computer operator, for example, only pays attention to the instrumental system at which she types when, as a result of malfunction or user error, the system presents itself as obstinate. When both she and it are functioning correctly she forgets it as she forgets her own body. When the whole ensemble is running smoothly, she gives no thought to her hands, to the keyboard, to the mouse, even to the screen at which she gazes. They all cease to be objects for her and become instead the transcended, surpassed moments of her overall project of operating the computer for whatever purpose.

A person's body is her consciousness in the sense that she is not in the world as a passive awareness, but as a being that acts towards the future. It can be said that her body is absorbed by her consciousness, so long as this is not taken in a dualistic sense to mean that body and consciousness are two distinct phenomena that happen to be united. To say that consciousness is embodied is not to say that consciousness happens to ride around inside the body like a driver in a car, but that embodiment is consciousness' way of being-in-the-world and its only way. The existence of each and every embodied person is unnecessary, accidental, contingent, but given that a person exists, it is absolutely necessary that she be embodied.

So far we have focused on the view of the body expressed by Heidegger and Sartre, but another existentialist philosopher who has some very interesting things to say about the body is Merleau-Ponty. Central to Merleau-Ponty's view is his opposition to the dualistic way of thinking that he says has characterised and misled western philosophy for centuries. He argues that the human condition, our way of being in the world, cannot be correctly understood or described until philosophy dispenses with such related dualisms as mind and body, subject and object, inner and outer. Merleau-Ponty increasingly came to realise that the main obstacle to dispensing with these dualisms is linguistic, that the very structure of language itself encourages dualistic ways of thinking.

The desire to overcome dualism is as central to Sartre's philosophy as it is to Merleau-Ponty's. Nonetheless, according to Merleau-Ponty, Sartre often slides into subject-object dualism as a result of the language he uses. An older, wiser, far more linguistically oriented Merleau-Ponty, even levelled the charge of dualism against himself, suggesting that his great early work, *Phenomenology of Perception*, had ultimately failed in its attempt to overcome dualism. Despite the retrospective claims of its author, it is generally held that the work in fact succeeds in extensively undermining the subject-object dichotomy through the detailed account it provides of the lived body or *body-subject*.

The term 'body-subject' identifies the subject, the person, *as* their body, rather than as an 'inner' that possesses a body as an 'outer'. The term also identifies the body as no mere object that can, for example, be moved away from oneself like other objects. Rather, the body *is* situation, perspective, perception, action, desire, intention and a host of other phenomena that comprise the self. 'I am my body,' Merleau-Ponty often says, echoing Sartre. To be embodied is not to *have* a body, but to *be* a body, and it is inconceivable to both Merleau-Ponty and Sartre that being a subject in the world could be achieved in any other way than by being a body.

Comparable though their views on embodiment are, Merleau-Ponty nonetheless criticises Sartre for falling into a dualistic way of thinking about embodiment and, more specifically, of underestimating the importance of embodiment in the experience of the Other as subject. As seen, in his theory of being-for-others, Sartre supposes that the Other must exist for me, as I must exist for the Other, as either transcendent subject or transcended object. The Other exists for me as a subject only when she transcends my transcendence and reduces me to an object.

The problem with this picture for Merleau-Ponty is that it ignores the fact that the Other exists for me most frequently as an embodied consciousness. That is, I am most often aware of the Other as a subject, not because my experience of my own embodiment indicates a subject who has transcended me, but because I experience a living, acting, embodied subject before me; a *subject incarnate*. I do not experience another person either as Other or as a body; her Otherness and her embodiment are given together as an utterly unified whole.

14 Love and Hate

In love, there is always one who kisses and one who offers the cheek.
(French Proverb)

Some of the great existentialists are famous for their many love affairs.
Nonetheless, as you might guess, the existentialists' view of so-called
romantic love is far from romantic. To begin with, in believing that
there are no abstract, metaphysical essences, that nothing exists beyond
particular things, they do not believe in love as a kind of power or force
that exists in its own right. 'Love is in the air' is not a phrase that
existentialists can allow themselves to take literally. Love is not a thing
but a deep desire for total unity with a particular Other, a desire to be
loved by a particular Other. The existentialists argue that the ideal of
love, total unity with the Other, is doomed to fail.

Actually, whether or not you think the existentialists' view of love is
romantic depends on what your idea of romance is. If your idea of
romance is Valentine's Day love-hearts and kisses, soft tone candlelit
dinners for two, big cuddly toys and walking hand in hand along the
beach at sunset, then it isn't romantic. If your idea of romance is somewhat more gothic and stormy, full of heartache, yearning and the thwarted
desire to possess; breaking up, making up and breaking up again, tears
before bedtime and tears in the rain, then maybe it is romantic.

So, romantic or erotic love is essentially Other related, and it is as an
aspect of being-for-others, as considered in Chapter 12, that existentialists

explore the phenomenon. The key question for them is: 'Why does the lover want to be loved?' To understand why it is that the lover wants to be loved is to understand what love is.

As you will know from your own experience, or from books and films in which the amorous tyrant imprisons her beloved, uneasily insisting, 'You will learn to love me', the lover is not satisfied with the mere physical possession of the Other. The lover may have contrived to have the Other physically close to her at all times, but if the lover does not possess the consciousness of the Other, if the Other does not choose to direct his consciousness towards the lover in a particular way, the lover will be deeply dissatisfied.

In desiring to possess the consciousness of the Other the lover does not want to enslave the Other. She does not want to possess a robot-thing whose passions flow mechanically in her direction, but a genuine Other who chooses at each moment to be possessed by her. The lover wants to be loved because she wants to possess the *freedom* of the Other. Not as an enslaved freedom that would no longer be a freedom, but as a freedom that remains free even though it is possessed, precisely because it continually *chooses* itself as possessed.

It is important to the lover that the choice to be possessed be constantly renewed by the Other. The lover will be dissatisfied with a love that continues to be given simply through loyalty to an oath, for example. Lovers are insecure and repeatedly demand pledges of love, yet lovers are nonetheless irritated by pledges because they want love to be determined by nothing but the freedom of the Other. The lover does not in fact even want to deliberately cause the Other to love her because a love that is deliberately caused by her is a love determined by something other than the freedom of the Other. Ideally, the lover wants to be loved by a freedom that is no longer free, not because this freedom has been enslaved or causally determined but because it continually enslaves itself and wills its own captivity.

Although lovers may pretend to a vast and noble unselfishness – 'I'll be there if you find you ever need me' – they are nothing if not demanding.

In wanting to possess the Other the lover wants to be nothing less than the whole world for the Other. She wants to be the meaning and purpose of the Other's world, that around which and for which the Other's entire world is ordered. The lover wants to be an object for the Other, but not the object that she is for those who do not love her, a mere being-in-the-midst-of-the-world alongside other objects, but a sacred object that symbolises the entire world for the Other and in which the freedom of the Other consents to lose itself.

The lover wants to be chosen as the limit of the Other's transcendence. She wants to be that towards which the Other transcends the entire world, without ever being that which the Other transcends. Ultimately, the lover wants to cease being a contingent and indeterminate person, subject to her own shifting evaluations and the evaluations of those who transcend her, and instead assume for herself the absolute, untranscendable value she believes she would have for the Other if only the Other chose to love her.

Romantic love is doomed, according to the existentialists, because what the lover wants is ultimately unachievable. It is impossible for the lover to possess the freedom of the Other while the Other remains free, because as soon as the Other loves the lover he experiences *her* as a subject and himself as an object confronted by her subjectivity. The lover wants to possess the transcendence of the Other as a transcendence while at the same time transcending it, but in taking possession of the transcendence of the Other she will inevitably negate it and reduce it to a facticity. Transcendence is always the transcendence of facticity. The lover can only transcend the Other as a facticity and not as a transcendence.

In seeking to take possession of the transcendence of the Other the lover runs the risk of being possessed by the transcendence of the Other, of being reduced to a facticity herself. The lover wants the freedom of the Other to elevate her to an absolute value, but she is playing with fire in that the freedom of the Other may suddenly look upon her with contempt or indifference and reduce her to an object amongst other objects.

It is important to stress that the lover is Other for the Other and that everything that has been said of the lover applies to the Other as well. The lover desires the Other to love her and thereby make her an absolute value. But if the Other loves the lover it is only because he wants her to make him an absolute value. Conflict, the essence of all human relationships according to some existentialists, is inevitable. To love is to want to be loved, so when one person loves another she does not in fact want, as the Other wants her to, to make the Other an absolute value. Instead, her love consists of wanting the Other to make her an absolute value.

The conclusion the existentialists draw about romantic love is that far from being the fine and generous emotion that it is often portrayed as, it is at heart *the demand to be loved*. Quite simply, as a pure demand, love can never supply what is demanded of it. The same dimensions and tensions manifest in romantic love are also manifest in what often constitutes the core of romantic love, namely *sexual desire*. Sexual desire is the theme of the next chapter. For now, I want to focus on that other great human passion, *hatred*.

Like romantic love and sexual desire, hatred is essentially Other related, it is yet another aspect of our being-for-others. The existentialists argue that any act on the part of the Other that puts a person in the state of being subject to the freedom and transcendence of the Other can arouse hatred. A person who is subjected to cruelty is likely to respond with hatred, but a person who is shown kindness may also respond with hatred rather than the expected gratitude. Both cruel acts and kind acts, in subjecting a person to the freedom of the Other, prevent that person from ignoring the Other.

Love, sexual desire, even masochism and sadism (see Chapter 15), aim at some form of union with the Other. Hatred, on the other hand, is the abandonment of any attempt to realise union with the Other. The person who hates does not want her freedom to be a transcendence of the Other, she wants to be free of the Other in a world where the Other does not exist. To hate is to pursue the death of the Other. This is not to say that hatred must involve actively plotting the death of the Other and usually it does not, otherwise murder would be far more common than it is. Rather, the person who hates seeks to realise for herself a world in which the hated Other does not feature and has no past, present or future significance. To hate is to want the death of the Other, but moreover it is to want that the Other had never existed in the first place.

Hatred should not be confused with contempt. Not least, there is often humour in contempt as displayed by ridicule. But hate, though it often struggles to disguise itself as contempt by pretending to laugh at the Other, takes the Other very seriously and is not at all amused. Hate does not abase the Other and to hate is not to have contempt for some particular aspect of the Other, such as his appearance. To hate is to resent the existence of the Other in general, with a certain grudging respect. Nietzsche writes: 'One does not hate so long as one continues to rate low, but only when one has come to rate equal or higher' (*Beyond Good and Evil*, 173, p. 179).

To hate the Other is to perceive him as an object, but the Other as a hate-object remains nonetheless an object haunted by a transcendence that the person who hates him prefers not to think about or acknowledge. This avoided transcendence lurks as a potential threat to the freedom of the person who hates. It threatens to alienate her and the hatred by means of which she strives to be free of the Other.

In hating, the person who hates strives to be free of the Other, strives to inhabit a world in which the Other does not exist and has never existed as a free transcendence. But the very fact that she hates the Other implies that she recognises the freedom of the Other. Hatred strives to deny the freedom of the Other by projecting the non-existence of the Other, but precisely because hatred is a striving to deny the Other it is an implicit affirmation of the Other.

Consistent with this analysis of hatred is the view that hatred fuels itself in so far as this implicit affirmation of the Other is given grudgingly and is therefore resented. She hates the Other all the more because her hatred of him obliges her to recognise his freedom. She blames the Other for the fact that her hatred of him cannot be the pure denial of him she wishes it to be.

Hatred fails as an attempt to abolish the Other because it cannot help being an implicit affirmation of the Other. Even if the hated Other dies or is killed by her he is not thereby abolished for her. Death does not make it that the Other had never existed, and for her hatred even to *attempt* to triumph in the death of the Other requires her to recognise that he *has* existed. She desires the death of the hated Other in order to be free of him, but with his death what she was for him becomes fixed in a past that she *is* as having-been-it. The fact that she cannot influence what she was for the Other once he is dead means that he continues to alienate her and to get the better of her from his grave.

Hatred is hatred of the Other as Other. As the hatred of otherness hatred is, arguably, hatred of all others in one Other. Hate is a person's revolt against her being-for-others in general. However, even if a person could entirely suppress or destroy all others, as tyrants attempt to do, she would not thereby reclaim her being-for-others or free herself from others. Once a person has been for others she will be forever haunted by her awareness that being-for-others is a permanent possibility of her being. To have been for-others is to have to be for-others for life.

It is worth noting that existentialists identify a further attitude towards other people that involves neither love nor hate. This attitude is *indifference*. Indifference is worth exploring in a chapter about love and hate because it provides an interesting contrast with love and hate that serves to shed further light upon them and upon the phenomenon of being-for-others in general. The overall conclusion, as you will see, is that it is far better to love or even to hate other people than to be indifferent towards them. To be indifferent is to be truly isolated and more or less dead inside.

The indifferent person is wilfully blind to the being of the Other as a transcendence and thereby to her own being-for-others. The indifferent person does in fact comprehend that the Other exists and that she is a being for the Other, but she practices evading this comprehension through a blindness maintained in bad faith. That is, she does not suffer her blindness as a state, she continually makes herself blind. She practices a sort of *solipsism*, acting as if she were alone in the world. 'Solipsism' is derived from the Latin words '*sōlus*' (alone) and '*ipse*' (self). 'Solipsism' literally means *self-alone-ism*. It is the philosophical theory that one's own mind is the only thing that exists.

She engages with the Other as an instrument or avoids the Other as an obstacle, recognising only the Other's function or lack of function. She refuses to imagine that the Other can *look* at her, that she can be an object for the Other's subjectivity, that the Other can render her a transcendence-transcended. She looks at the Other's look only as a modification of the mechanism that the Other is for her, as something that expresses what the Other is rather than what she is for the Other. She certainly does not look at the Other's look to stare the Other down and render him a transcendence-transcended. She has perfected a studied indifference towards the transcendence of the Other and has no interest in a battle of wills with the Other.

The indifferent person appears to have discovered a way of no longer being threatened by the Other's transcendence, but in fact it is because she is so threatened by the Other's transcendence that she persists in her indifference. As she is indifferent to the Other, she cannot be shy, timid or embarrassed before the Other, and so comes across as self-confident. But her self-confidence is not a confidence before the Other as Other – she will not allow the Other to exist for her in that way. It is rather a confidence in her practiced ability to manage the instrument or obstacle that the Other is for her.

Indifference, then, is premised upon a deep insecurity and involves a profound isolation. The indifferent person is alienated by her alienation of the Other. In cutting herself off from the Other she is cut off from what she could be for the Other and from what the Other could make her be.

Her indifference to the transcendence of the Other means that she can neither transcend the Other's transcendence to become a subject for the Other, or be transcended by the transcendence of the Other to become an object for the Other. She can only be the unjustifiable subjectivity that she is for herself. She is stuck with herself, unable to find any relief from her ambiguity, indeterminacy and contingency in what the Other makes of her, in the evaluations he imposes on her.

Sartre, as seen, famously argues that 'Hell is other people' (*In Camera*, p. 223), meaning that it is hell to exist for the Other and to be at the mercy of the Other's judgements. This analysis of indifference, however, which Sartre fully endorses, recognises the deeper hell of refusing to exist for the Other and of isolating oneself in one's own subjectivity.

Being-for-others is undoubtedly a source of distress, but it is also a source of solace and pleasure. Only by acknowledging the existence of the Other, and in so doing her existence for the Other, can a person feel proud or flattered, for example. In allowing herself to be reduced to an object by the Other's look she may be pleased to discover that she is a pleasant or fascinating object for the Other and so on. The Other is a source of positive as well as negative evaluations, but the Other cannot be a source of *any* evaluations unless his otherness is admitted.

15   Sexual Desire

'Oh don't, Boris, please. Sex without love is an empty experience.'
'Yes, but as empty experiences go, it's one of the best.'
(Woody Allen, *Love and Death*, 1975)

Existentialists view sexual desire as a phenomenon that can be broken down and analysed, subjected to what they call a *phenomenological reduction*. This view is opposed to that of Freudian psychoanalysis which treats sexual desire as irreducible, as a fundamental given that must be used as a basis for explaining almost everything else about human behaviour.

Existentialists are critical of any theory that attempts to explain people in terms of what they call *pseudo-irreducible* drives and desires. The existential psychoanalyst, R. D. Laing, argues that to explain a person in terms of pseudo-irreducible drives and desires reduces her to those drives and desires and hence explains her away. Existentialists explore the phenomenon of sexual desire as yet another aspect of being-for-others, and it is in viewing sexual desire as an aspect of being-for-others that they succeed in breaking it down and analysing it.

Sexual desire is not simply sexual instinct. A person could not experience sexual desire (or anything else) if she did not have a body, and sexual desire very much involves the body, but sexual desire is not generated by the body, or more specifically the sex organs, as a demand for sex, orgasm or procreation. Viewed objectively, sexual desire appears as an appetite like hunger that seeks satisfaction from a particular object. From the internal perspective of consciousness or being-for-itself, however, sexual desire differs radically from hunger.

Hunger is a physiological urge that a person becomes conscious of. Hunger is *for* consciousness in so far as to be hungry is to be conscious of being hungry, but hunger, unlike sexual desire, is not a state or condition of consciousness. Sexual desire, on the other hand, unlike hunger, is a radical modification of consciousness that troubles consciousness and defines it to its core. Sexual desire is consciousness itself 'hungry' for a certain relationship with the body of the Other that will bring about a certain relationship with its own body.

Sexual desire is an attempt to make the Other exist as flesh for the one who desires and for the Other himself. In the terms of Sartre and others, sexual desire is an attempt to realise the *incarnation* of the body of the Other as flesh. But, critics will ask, isn't the Other already incarnated, given that the Other is made of flesh? Certainly, the Other's body is made of flesh, but as we have seen, it is not primarily as an object that the Other exists for himself or for others. The Other's flesh is usually concealed, not only by his clothes but by his movements. Even a person who is naked can conceal his flesh as mere flesh with movements that are sufficiently graceful. The Other is not flesh but rather a being in action who transcends his body towards his possibilities.

Sexual desire aims to divest the Other's body of its actions, its transcendence and its possibilities, so as to reveal the inertia and passivity of the Other's body to him and to the one who desires him. This divesting and revealing is achieved through the sexual caress which, through the pleasure it gives the Other, causes the Other to become his flesh for himself and for the one who caresses.

It is possible for a person to caress the Other with her eyes alone. To look at the Other with desire is to caress him and incarnate him as flesh. The person who caresses does so to reveal the Other as flesh, but she does not want her caressing to take hold of him or to act upon him. Instead, she wants her caressing to be a passive placing of her body against the Other's body. She wants the very gentleness and passivity of her caresses to reveal her own passive flesh to the Other and to herself. She desires to caress the Other's body in such a way that in caressing the Other's body she is caressed by the Other's body.

The person who caresses seeks to incarnate the Other as flesh so as to incarnate herself as flesh, and to incarnate herself as flesh so as to incarnate the Other as flesh. She makes the Other enjoy her flesh through his flesh so as to compel him to be his flesh and so on.

This is what existentialists call *double reciprocal incarnation*. Ultimately, sexual desire is the desire for double reciprocal incarnation. To achieve double reciprocal incarnation would be to possess the Other's transcendent freedom as an incarnated consciousness by possessing the flesh that the Other's transcendent freedom has determined itself to be. Like romantic love, with which it is closely associated, sexual desire aims at the unachievable possession of the Other's transcendence as a transcendence rather than as a transcendence-transcended.

We saw in the previous chapter that the ultimate goal of romantic love, possession of the Other's transcendence as a transcendence, is unachievable. Similarly, the ultimate goal of sexual desire, double reciprocal incarnation, is also impossible to achieve. A person cannot at the same time incarnate the Other's body and be incarnated by the Other's body. If the Other's body incarnates her body she will become lost in the enjoyment of her own incarnation. Her own incarnation will become the object of her consciousness and she will forget or neglect the incarnation of the Other. Sexual desire is the desire for a mutual caress, but caressing, for all its striving after the mutual caress, remains touching and being touched. As the old saying goes, 'There is always one who kisses and one who is kissed.'

Ironically perhaps, it is pleasure itself that brings about the failure of the ideal of sexual desire. The more a person feels sexual pleasure in the incarnation of her own body by the Other, the less she will focus on her desire for the Other. In focusing on her own sexual pleasure she will lose sight of the Other as Other and no longer strive to possess him as an incarnated consciousness.

The failure of sexual desire to achieve its ultimate goal of reciprocal incarnation almost inevitably leads to the emergence of some level of sadomasochism. Sadism and masochism are rocky reefs upon which the ship of sexual desire has a tendency to founder. Indeed, sexual desire founders so often and so readily upon these reefs that 'normal' sexuality is *sadistic-masochistic*.

With regard to sadism, as soon as a person neglects her own incarnation and focuses on the incarnation of the Other, as soon as she surpasses the facticity of her own body towards the possibility of acting on the Other, of *taking* the Other, she has already oriented herself in the direction of sadism.

With regard to masochism, as soon as a person neglects the incarnation of the Other and focuses on her own incarnation, as soon as she wants to be constituted as a facticity for the transcendence of the Other, to be acted on by the Other and *taken* by the Other, she has already oriented herself in the direction of masochism.

Let's look more closely at sadism and masochism.

Sadism, like masochism, emerges when sexual desire fails to achieve its goal of reciprocal incarnation. As said, a person whose sexual desire is not sadistic wants to exist as flesh for herself and for the Other. She also wants the Other to exist as flesh for himself and for her. She wants to achieve that elusive holy grail of sexual desire, a double reciprocal incarnation of the flesh. The sadist, however, does not want to achieve a double reciprocal incarnation, or is incapable of doing so. She may have a horror of her own incarnation and consider it a humiliating state.

The sadist refuses to be incarnated while at the same time seeking to possess the incarnation of the Other. She denies her own facticity in her efforts to transcend the Other and possess the facticity of the Other. As the sadist refuses to incarnate the Other through her own incarnation, she must incarnate the Other by using him as a tool. To make a tool of the Other is to make an object of the Other, and it is as an *instrument-object* that the sadist wants the Other to realise his incarnation.

To understand sadism it helps to contrast the graceful with the ungraceful or obscene. A graceful body that has poise and moves with ease and precision is an instrument that manifests a person's freedom. A person who is naked conceals the facticity and obscenity of her flesh if her movements are sufficiently graceful. An ungraceful or obscene body, on the other hand, one that lacks poise and is awkward and laboured in its movements, is an instrument that manifests a person's facticity.

An ungraceful, naked body is, so to speak, more naked and obscene than a graceful naked body for not being clothed in grace. It is the obscene body, the instrument-object that manifests facticity, rather than the graceful body that manifests freedom, that the sadist desires to incarnate. Sadism aims to destroy grace because it is a manifestation of the Other's freedom. The more ungraceful the sadist can make the body of the Other, through the pain she inflicts and the humiliating postures she forces the Other to adopt, the more she will feel that she has enslaved the Other's freedom.

Pain is a facticity that invades consciousness. It is through the pain that the sadist inflicts on the Other that she forces the Other to identify himself with the facticity of his flesh. The sadist uses violence to force the Other into an *incarnation through pain*. In pain the Other is incarnated for himself and for the sadist. The sadist enjoys the possession of the Other's flesh that she achieves through violence whilst also enjoying her own non-incarnation.

In her state of non-incarnation the sadist is a free transcendence, she is all action, she feels powerful as she skilfully brings instruments of torture to bear upon the body of the Other in order to capture the freedom of the Other in pained flesh. The consciousness of the Other is ensnared in pain and as the sadist is the cause of this pain she feels she has ensnared the freedom of the Other. Sadism, however, like love, sexual desire and masochism, like all attempts to gain possession of the freedom of the Other, is doomed to failure.

The sadist wants to incarnate the flesh of the Other by using the Other as an instrument, but to apprehend the body as an instrument is very different from apprehending it as flesh. Instruments refer to other instruments, to a system of instrumentality. They are utilisable, they have potential, they indicate the future. Flesh revealed as flesh is an unutilisable facticity without potential, it is simply there in its contingency and superfluity referring to nothing beyond itself. The sadist can utilise the flesh of the Other as an instrument to reveal flesh, but as soon as the flesh *is* revealed in all its unutilisable facticity, no instrument remains for the sadist to possess through utilisation.

The sadist strives for possession by utilisation, but her very utilisation of the flesh of the Other eventually incarnates flesh that cannot be utilised and, therefore, does not allow possession by utilisation. The sadist realises her failure to possess the Other at the very moment she achieves complete mastery over the Other, because in mastering the Other and reducing him to pained, contingent flesh, to a non-instrument, there is nothing left for her to utilise.

The sadist could utilise the flesh of the Other to satisfy herself sexually, to achieve orgasm through intercourse and so on, but as this would involve the incarnation of her own flesh by the flesh of the Other it would not be sadism as defined. As noted, the non-incarnation of the flesh of the sadist is central to the phenomenon of sadism. In giving way to the desire for the incarnation of her own flesh she would cease to be sadistic. It is always possible that the project of sadism will be undermined by the emergence of desire within the sadist for the incarnation of her own flesh. As Sartre says, 'Sadism is the failure of desire, and desire is the failure of sadism' (*Being and Nothingness*, pp. 426–427).

The project of sadism also fails because the freedom of the Other that the sadist strives to possess remains out of reach. The sadist's actions aim at recovering her being-for-others, but the more she acts upon the Other, torturing and inflicting pain, the more the Other slips away from her into his consciousness of being assaulted. The Other is not a being she has possessed but a being lost to her in his preoccupation with his own suffering.

The sadist discovers the failure of her sadism most acutely when the Other looks at her and thereby transcends her transcendence. As a transcendence-transcended she experiences herself as an object for the subjectivity of the Other. The look of the Other alienates her freedom and reduces her to a being-in-the-midst-of-the-world. The mere gaze of the Other triumphs over all her sadistic violence and cruelty.

She may attempt identification with the Other by surrendering her freedom to his and allowing him to possess her as an object. This new attempt to identify with the Other is masochistic. A person who resorts to masochism will attempt to become for the Other a mere object without subjectivity. She will attempt to engage herself wholly in her objective being. She will attempt to deny her transcendence with the intention of becoming a pure facticity for the transcendence of the Other.

The masochist wants to become a transcendence-transcended by the Other to the extent that her transcendence is utterly annihilated by the freedom of the Other. As a mere object for the Other she will feel ashamed but she will love her shame as the measure of her objectivity. The more ashamed, naked, helpless and debased the masochist becomes before the Other, the more of an object she will feel herself to be.

In desiring to be an object for the Other, the masochist desires to be an object for herself. In fact, she wants to be an object for the Other in order to satisfy her desire to be an object for herself. The masochist does not in fact attempt to fascinate the Other with her objectivity, rather she attempts to fascinate herself with her objectivity for the Other. Masochism may appear even to the masochist as a final and utterly selfless attempt to fascinate the Other through a total surrender to the Other, but in so far as the masochist aims ultimately to fascinate herself with her objectivity for the Other she is acting selfishly and, indeed, using the Other.

The masochist wants to be constituted as a facticity by the Other so as to experience her own transcendence as nothing. The masochist's project of seeking to be for herself the mere object that she is for the Other is, not least, a project of seeking to escape the anxiety she feels as a free transcendence burdened with having to make choices. As an attempted renunciation of transcendence, masochism is a form of bad faith.

Masochism is and must be doomed to failure. To attempt to fascinate herself with her objectivity for the Other the masochist must be conscious of herself as an object for the Other. If she is conscious of herself as an object, however, then she is not that object but rather the transcendence of that object. She can only aim at being the object she is for the Other through a transcendence that always places her at a distance from being the object she is for the Other. The harder she tries to be her objectivity, the more she will assert her subjectivity. Furthermore, her project of fascinating herself with her objectivity for the Other actually uses the Other as an instrument.

If a masochist pays a man to tie her up and whip her, he becomes her instrument. She treats him as an object and hence is in transcendence in relation to him.

16 Marriage

Hitherto we had not even considered the possibility of submitting ourselves to the common customs and observances of our society, and in consequence the notion of getting married had simply not crossed our minds. It offended our principles. (Simone de Beauvoir, *The Prime of Life*, p. 76)

Marriage is so central to so many people's life experience and journey that it must surely be included in a guide that explores the essential, existential features of the human condition. Unlike birth, however, which is unavoidable for the person born, or death which is ultimately inevitable, marriage is not in fact an essential feature of the human condition.

Lots of people don't marry or even cohabitate as though they were married. Some people make a choice to remain single while others are simply never confronted with marriage related choices. Unlike birth, death, time, being-for-others and so on, which are existential givens in face of which all people must choose themselves, marriage is a convention, a construction, that need not necessarily figure in a person's life at all.

Of course, because the convention of marriage is so widespread people often find themselves having to make serious, life defining choices with regard to it: to marry or to stay single, to marry this or that person, to marry for love or money, to stay married and so on. Marriage is perhaps the single most significant human convention there is, but still it is not a fundamental given of human existence. Marriage is a bit like Christmas, an artificial construction that so dominates events that most people are obliged to make choices with regard to it whether they want to or not.

As previously argued, in love the Other *chooses* to be possessed and can therefore abandon this choice at any time. The love the Other gives is always subject to his *freedom*. This makes the lover, whose desire is to be loved, insecure. Despite her insecurity, however, the lover wants the love of the Other to be given freely, because a love that is not freely given is not love. Marriage appears to offer the perfect solution to this dilemma.

The *ideal* of marriage is that it should secure love once and for all, happily ever after, while also preserving the freedom from which all true love must flow. Marriage appears to offer a gilt-edged *guarantee* that the love of the Other will always continue to be freely given and never withdrawn or given to another. So lovers make their solemn vows before family, friends and God, seeking to cement with rings and rituals oaths that can only ever have the value their makers choose to give them at any time in the future.

High divorce and adultery rates are testament to the fact that commitment is nothing in itself, that it consists entirely in the constant reaffirmation of a certain choice set against the ever present, lurking possibility of a change of mind. Existentialists tend to view marriage as a somewhat desperate attempt to transform the love of the Other into something fixed, reliable and certain, precisely because love isn't something fixed, reliable and certain.

In many cases marriage certainly supplies the conditions in which true love can thrive. Shared interests arise from a shared daily life while other would-be lovers are formally excluded. Not least, there is ample opportunity for intimacy and mutual reassurance, set against reduced opportunity and incentive to betray the relationship on a mere passing whim. 'Marriage', as George Bernard Shaw notes, 'combines the maximum of temptation with the maximum of opportunity' (*Man and Superman*, p. 510).

In many other cases, however, marriage steadily undermines love as the basis of the relationship shifts from being a free choice by the Other to be possessed, towards mere habit, ingratitude, fear of change and material and financial entanglement. As the comedian Bob Monkhouse once joked, 'I'd never be unfaithful to my wife, I love my house too much.'

In championing freedom above all else, existentialists stress that all personal relationships should be based on freedom. That is, they should be entered into freely and maintained as a matter of mutual, ongoing choice. Hence, existentialists would certainly disapprove of any marriage that was arranged or coerced or where either party felt obliged to enter into it for fear of the consequences of not doing so.

Existentialism eventually led Simone de Beauvoir to feminism. In her most important and controversial work, *The Second Sex*, a work that heralded a feminist revolution, she considers the secondary role assigned to women by society. She argues that the position of most women throughout history has been one of dependency upon men. Thanks partly to the feminist movement, matters have improved somewhat in some places. Some women have the economic independence that de Beauvoir argues is so vital to personal independence. Nonetheless, it remains the case that millions of women the world over are without freedom in any real, practical sense. Their existential freedom remains inalienable, they cannot not choose, but their freedom does not amount to much if their only choice is between starvation and entering into a marriage where they are little more than the property of their husband.

Undoubtedly, there is often mutual love, affection and respect in such marriages but these qualities are a fortuitous bonus to the marriage rather than its *raison d'être*. Of course, it is also true that many marriages *entered into* on the grounds of mutual love persist when that love has utterly gone and divorce would be a blessed relief to all. As Woody Allen says in the film, *Play it Again, Sam*, 'My parents never got divorced, although I begged them to.' The reasons why such marriages persist are complex, but certainly in most cases material entanglement, habit and even stubbornness play no small part.

The overall existentialist position regarding marriage is something like this: marriage entered into as a result of social expectation coercion, obligation, fear, poverty etc. is entirely at odds with the existentialist ethic of individual freedom. Marriage entered into in the absence of any determining factors other than mutual love, affection and respect is okay if such a 'marriage of true minds' (Shakespeare, 'Sonnet 116') is ever possible. But not marrying at all, or even cohabitating, is by far the best option.

Paradoxically, in the existentialists' view, true love is only possible when both parties remain *single* and make no emotional claims upon one another. As love is only love if it is given freely then a genuine loving relationship can be based on nothing else but freedom. A relationship can only hope to remain genuinely loving by preserving the conditions that keep it free and avoiding the conditions that would tie it down. This inevitably means being uncomplaining if the beloved has intimate relations with others. As the true existentialist makes no claims upon her beloved in the first place, it would be incorrect to say that she *allows* him to have affairs. He is simply free to have affairs without reproach if he wants to, openly and honestly, and must not be made to feel the need to deceive anyone.

Having spent years teaching in the provinces, Sartre and de Beauvoir finally obtained teaching posts in Paris. They had been lovers for a long time, despite or because of their various affairs, and the predictable thing for them to do was to get a place together. Indeed, the respectable, bourgeois thing for them to do at the age they had now reached was to 'tie the knot' and get married. But despising the predictable and the bourgeois, and viewing them as pretty much indistinguishable, they remained single and took up separate accommodation in the same hotel, a move that preserved the vitality of their relationship by preserving its essential freedom. As de Beauvoir writes: 'Sartre lived on the floor above me; thus we had all the advantages of a shared life, without any of its inconveniences' (*The Prime of Life*, p. 315).

Throughout their lives and their lifelong relationship Sartre and de Beauvoir maintained that marriage is basically a bourgeois institution that seeks to bind people into an intimate association that ought, instead, to be freely chosen day by day.

Lovers should resist the false security offered by marriage vows and material entanglements and accept that the love they currently enjoy is based, and can only be based, on nothing more than the freedom of the Other. To live like this may well be a source of great anxiety, but anxiety is the price of freedom. The true existentialist would rather endure anxiety than seek in bad faith to impose artificial and stifling limits on her own freedom and her lover's freedom simply for the sake of her peace of mind.

17 Emotions

The greater the feeling of inferiority that has been experienced, the more powerful is the urge for conquest and the more violent the emotional agitation. (Alfred Adler, *The Neurotic Constitution*, p. 16)

In examining being-for-others we have already explored a significant amount of the existentialist theory of emotion. Existentialists recognise that much of a person's emotional life is Other related; that many if not most of a person's emotions are different ways in which she encounters the Other and realises herself as a being for the Other.

How much of an emotional life does a solitary person actually have or need? Perhaps the so-called emotion of elation that people feel when enjoying solitude well away from other people is not so much an emotion as a sense of freedom from emotion; a transcendence of cloying, irksome Other related feelings like self-consciousness, shame, embarrassment, anger, repulsion and disappointment.

It will be objected that not all these are necessarily Other related emotions. Disappointment, for example, is not necessarily an Other related emotion in the sense that a person can be disappointed by non-personal things like the weather. But surely, most of the disappointment people experience in their lives is due to others, just as most of the anger and irritation they experience is due to others, or more specifically, their *reaction* to others. Other people disappoint and anger us so readily precisely because we have so many practical and emotional requirements with regard to them, requirements they seldom want to fully satisfy. Other people are nothing to us if not frustrating.

As for the emotion of loneliness that the solitary person may feel, what is this emotion but a hankering after engagement with the Other? A person often feels loneliest when she has recently been in contact with the Other, especially if that contact ended before she had her fill of it. She feels the Other's lack and so misses the Other. When a person has been alone for some time, however, the lack of the Other tends to diminish as she chooses new paths of transcendence that are not dependent on the Other.

Returning to an empty house after a night out with friends, Jane always feels isolated and lonely for half an hour or so. Yet, spending a whole busy week alone in the same house she never feels isolated or lonely and doesn't miss other people at all. The once empty house is now full of her, as she is full of herself.

We often get very emotional when angry, disappointed or frustrated with ourselves. But arguably, to be angry with ourselves is always to be angry with ourselves as Other. I am performing some task and become angry with myself when I make a mess of it. The present me is angry with the me I was a moment ago for messing up and costing the present me precious time and effort to put things right.

In cursing my stupidity I curse my former self for impeding the anticipated transcendence of my present self, for causing me to suddenly find this situation, which I was smoothly transcending towards larger and more important future goals, an oppressive nuisance. Is there any need or room for what we call 'emotion' when we are thoroughly absorbed in a task and our transcendence is smooth? Shortly, we will look at the view that emotion occurs when a situation, a task, at least temporarily, becomes too difficult for a person to cope with.

Interestingly, existentialists argue that emotions are not actually states of being that we posses or that possess us. Rather, we must always aim at a particular emotion without ever being able to be at one with it. As essentially ambiguous and indeterminate beings, it is never possible for us to become anything in the mode of being it. We can only ever aim at what we are, play at what we are and so on. It is therefore impossible for a person to achieve an emotional state such that they become unified with that emotional state.

The sad person, for example, strives to be in herself what in actual fact she must make herself be. Initially, the claim that a sad person is not sad in the mode of *being* sad is likely to meet with greater resistance than the claim that we are not identical with what we do. The fact that a banker so evidently plays at being a banker is sufficient to reveal that he is not really a banker in the mode of being one. Surely though, if a person is sad then she is sad in the mode of being what she is; surely she is to be identified with her emotional state. To hold the view that a person is identical with her emotional state, however, is to fail to grasp that consciousness is always other than itself and never self-identical. The nature of consciousness implies that there is no such *thing* as an emotional state.

In everyday life it is not misleading to speak of a person being in a certain emotional state. When, in an everyday situation, a person behaving hysterically is described as being 'in an hysterical state', the intention is simply to convey an image of a distraught person who is screaming, crying and tearing at her hair. Many psychologists, however, are misled by such talk. Believing that mental and emotional phenomena have a certain objective existence, they take the expression literally and go in search of the state of hysteria in itself; its psychological and physiological essence. But hysteria has no essence; hysteria *is* hysterical behaviour.

What is true of temporary emotional states like hysteria is also true of enduring mental conditions like schizophrenia. Criticising traditional psychology, R. D. Laing points out that having a mental condition like schizophrenia is not like having a cold. 'No one *has* schizophrenia, like having a cold. The patient has not 'got' schizophrenia. He is schizophrenic' (*The Divided Self*, p. 34).

Psychologists will object that many emotional states do have at least a physiological essence. Tourette's syndrome, for example, which is characterised by sudden, repetitive movements and utterances, is the result of certain neurochemical irregularities in the brain. However, that a person is subject by virtue of the facticity of her biology to involuntary spasms of aggressive behaviour, to a failure of aggression inhibition, does not mean that within her biology there exists the substantial being-in-itself of aggression. Although the Tourette's sufferer behaves aggressively due to physiological causes beyond her control, and is not, therefore, responsible for her actions, her aggression can no more be separated from her behaviour than a university can be separated from the buildings and functions that comprise it.

There is no such *thing* as sadness. The sad person is not a sad thing in the way that a crow is a black thing. Sadness is rather the transcendent meaning of a certain set of gestures; the meaning of a certain slumped, listless demeanour. As sadness is nothing but the meaning of postures that a person must re-adopt moment by moment, she cannot take possession of her sadness. She can no more take possession of her sadness and be united with it than she can be united with herself.

Sadness is not a being but a conduct; the conduct of a person who makes herself sad. The requirement of having to be perpetually at a distance from herself in order to make herself sad means that she can never be sad in the manner of being what she is. As Sartre says, 'If I make myself sad, it is because I am not sad – the being of the sadness escapes me by and in the very act by which I affect myself with it' (*Being and Nothingness*, p. 84).

A person cannot give sadness to herself as she can give a gift to another. Precisely because she exists as that which always *strives* to be fixed and substantial, she cannot *be* fixed and substantial. In so far as her being is to be what she is not, she is sad only in so far as she makes herself sad and reflects upon herself as sad. Her sadness is not an object in consciousness reflected on; it exists entirely in and through an act of self-reflection.

The sadness of another, especially when portrayed in art, theatre or film, appears to a person to have more substance than her own. As her sadness consists only in an irresolute commitment to be sad she may envy the sadness of others in so far as their sadness appears to her to be sadness in itself. She too would like to be the personification of sadness: a weeping, dejected angel of melancholia pictured by an artist. Far from wanting to snap out of her sadness, she will want, for example, to honour a lost lover with a sadness that is the epitome of despair. Or, in bad faith, she will strive to become her sadness and despair in order to escape her freedom to hope that her lover will return; a hope that tortures her with apprehension as it repeatedly raises her up only to cast her down. However, because sadness is only the conduct of a person who makes herself sad, she can never, so to speak, be sad enough.

This view of sadness reveals the full extent to which, according to Sartre, 'Man is a useless passion' (*Being and Nothingness*, p. 636). Each person is such a useless passion that she must despair even of becoming, as a last desperate means of escaping her free transcendence, a being in despair in the mode of being what she is.

Sartre's position echoes that of Kierkegaard. In *The Sickness unto Death*, Kierkegaard considers a girl who despairs over the loss of her lover: 'Just try now, just try saying to such a girl, "You are consuming yourself," and you will hear her answer, "O, but the torment is simply that I cannot do that"' (*The Sickness unto Death*, p. 50). The girl has to be herself as despairing, rather than escape herself by having herself consumed by despair. She despairs of being at one with her despair as a means of escaping her consciousness of despair.

In 1939 Sartre published a book called *Sketch for a Theory of the Emotions*. Although very short, this book contains many powerful insights into the nature of emotion that are well worth exploring.

In *Sketch for a Theory of the Emotions* Sartre advocates a philosophical method of investigating emotion as opposed to a psychological one. The phenomenon of emotion, he argues, can only be properly understood by subjecting it to a *phenomenological reduction* that thoroughly analyses it and grasps its true essence.

The problem with psychology, as opposed to phenomenology, is that it fails to grasp the essential features of phenomena and instead simply lists facts about phenomena that appear as accidental. Psychologists can only say that there is emotion, that it involves certain behaviours in certain situations. They cannot explain why there is emotion, what it signifies or why it is an essential aspect of human consciousness and a necessary feature of human reality.

Psychologists investigate people in situation, but phenomenology investigates what it is for people to be situated. Emotion is an inalienable feature of human situatedness and human reality, it belongs essentially to our way of being in the world and is not the accidental addition to human reality that psychology makes it appear.

Sartre offers psychology the insights of phenomenology in the hope that psychology will derive a method from phenomenology that will enable it to do more than simply accumulate observational data that it hopes to interpret in future through the accumulation of yet more data. Pure psychology underpinned by phenomenological psychology would be able to comprehend the essential significance of psychological phenomena by identifying them as aspects of a coherent whole. Pure psychology, that great, barren, reductionist, pseudo-science that enthrals the masses by pretending to have the power to help people understand each other *as people*, has, as yet, largely failed to take up Sartre's generous offer.

In moving towards an account of his own phenomenological theory of emotions, Sartre begins by critically examining the classic theories of emotion put forward by William James, Pierre Janet and Tamara Dembo respectively.

James endorses the *peripheric* theory of emotions, arguing that emotion is consciousness of physiological manifestations. A person feels sad, for example, because she weeps, rather than vice versa. If emotion was simply awareness of physiological manifestations, however, then different emotions could not be associated with the same physiological manifestations in the way that they are. Weeping accompanies relief as well as sadness and the fact that the physiological manifestations of joy and anger differ only in intensity does not mean that anger is a greater intensity of joy. The central weakness of the peripheric theory is that it overlooks the fact that an emotion is first and foremost consciousness of feeling that emotion and not simply consciousness of weeping or laughing; it has *meaning*, it is a certain way or relating to the world.

Janet's theory is an improvement on James' as it recognises that emotion is not simply an awareness of physiological disturbance but a *behaviour*. Janet views emotion as a behaviour of defeat that serves to reduce tension. For example, a girl breaks down in tears rather than discuss her case with her doctor.

Sartre agrees with Janet that emotion is a behaviour of defeat, but criticises him for not appreciating that defeated behaviour can only be such if consciousness has conferred that meaning upon it through its awareness of the possibility of an alternative, superior, undefeated behaviour. For Janet, the girl simply begins to cry as an automatic reaction to the situation in which she finds herself. For Sartre, the girl's action is and must be deliberate. She cries in order to avoid talking to the doctor, although in bad faith she refuses to recognise that this is her motive or indeed that she has any motive.

Dembo, whose theory is closest to Sartre's own, holds that emotion is an inferior response to a situation that may occur when a superior response has failed. For example, a person becomes angry and kicks the machine she has failed to fix. Sartre agrees with Dembo that emotion is an inferior response to a situation that occurs when a superior response has failed, but argues that Dembo fails to acknowledge the significance of the role played by consciousness in the change of response. One form of behaviour cannot replace another unless consciousness presents the new behaviour to itself as a possible, if inferior, alternative to the present behaviour.

To summarise: all three classic theories of emotion are inadequate because they fail to recognise or sufficiently acknowledge the essential role that consciousness and intention play in the emotions

Sartre moves on to critically examine the psychoanalytic theory of emotion put forward by Freud and his followers. Arguing for a position that has become central to the theory and practice of *existential* psychoanalysis, Sartre contends that the traditional psychoanalytic distinction between consciousness and the unconscious, the domain of primitive drives and desires, is nonsensical in various ways.

In *Being and Nothingness* he argues that the ego would actually have to be conscious of the memories and desires it was imprisoning in the subconscious, the memories and desires it was *repressing*, in order to act as a discerning censor. 'In a word, how could the censor discern the impulses needing to be repressed without being conscious of discerning them?' (*Being and Nothingness,* p. 76). In *Sketch for a Theory of the Emotions* he questions the very possibility of a relationship between consciousness and an unconscious.

For Freudian psychoanalysis, emotion is a phenomenon of consciousness, but *essentially* it is 'the symbolic realization of a desire repressed by the censor' (*Sketch for a Theory of the Emotions*, p. 51). The desire, being repressed, plays no part in its symbolic realization as an emotion. The emotion, then, despite the claims of Freudian psychoanalysis, is only what it appears to consciousness to be, anger, fear and so on. Freudian psychoanalysis considers emotion to be a signifier of whatever lurks in the unconscious, but as Sartre points out, the signifier is entirely cut off from what is signified.

Freudian psychoanalysis, argues Sartre, treats consciousness as a passive phenomenon, receiving and being the signification of meanings from outside without even knowing what they mean. But consciousness, as we have seen, is not a passive phenomenon. It is entirely active, it makes itself, it is nothing but consciousness of being conscious of the world. As such, whatever meanings consciousness signifies are its own meanings, meanings *for* consciousness, not meanings that are received from 'behind' or 'beneath' consciousness that have no meaning for consciousness.

The great error of Freudian psychoanalysis is that it interrogates consciousness from the outside, treating it as a passive collection of signs, indicators and traces that have their meaning and significance elsewhere. In fundamentally misrepresenting the nature of conscious- ness psychoanalysis overlooks the fact that the significance of emotion lies within consciousness, that consciousness is itself 'the *signification and what is signified*' (*Sketch for a Theory of the Emotions*, p. 53). Phenomenology, unlike Freudian psychoanalysis, undertakes to interrogate consciousness itself – as a relation to the world and to itself – for the meaning of emotion.

In outlining his own view of emotion, Sartre argues that although people can always consciously reflect on their emotions, emotion is not originally or primarily a phenomenon of reflection, a state of mind. Emotional consciousness, argues Sartre, is first and foremost conscious- ness *of* the world. Emotions are intentional, they are a way of appre- hending the world. For every emotion there is the object of that emotion, every emotion is directedness towards its object and exists as a relationship with its object. The emotional person and the object of her emotion are wholly bound together. To be frightened is to be afraid *of* something, to be angry is to be angry *with* something, to be joyful is to be joyful *about* something and so on.

Sartre considers the kind of relationship to the world that emotion is and what is common to all the diverse occasions when emotion occurs. The world presents itself as a system of instrumentality that people utilize to achieve their goals. There is always a degree of diffi- culty involved in utilizing any system, always the possibility of obstacles and pitfalls arising that hinder progress. Difficulty manifests itself as a quality of the world itself. Sartre describes objects as *exigent*, they are exacting and demanding, their potentialities can only be realised by overcoming certain difficulties. Emotion occurs when the world becomes too difficult for a person to cope with.

Finding all ways of acting in the instrumental world barred by diffi- culty, a person spontaneously and non-reflectively wills the transforma- tion of the world from a world governed by causal processes to a world governed by *magic* where causal processes no longer apply. Emotion is a spontaneous attitude to a situation that aims to magically transform that situation in such a way that it suddenly no longer presents an insurmountable difficulty or threat to the consciousness of the person concerned.

A person faced with great danger, for example, may faint as a means of removing that danger from her conscious grasp, even though fainting does not normally serve to remove a danger in any real, practical sense. Similarly, a person may angrily curse, hit or throw a tool that is proving difficult or impossible to utilise, as though the world had magically become a place where the difficulty presented by a tool could be removed by these 'means'.

In Sartre's view, all emotions are functional. Anger is evidently functional but, on the face of it, joy does not seem to fit this description. Unlike an angry or frightened person, surely a joyful person does not need to magically transform her situation; surely she wants her situation to be as it is with its object or source of joy secured? Sartre distinguishes emotional joy from the joyful feeling that results from adapting to the world and achieving temporary equilibrium with it.

Emotional joy occurs precisely because the object or source of joy is not yet secured and if it is secured will only be obtained by degrees and never as an instantaneous totality. Sartre considers a man who is told that he has won a large sum of money. The man is restless with joy in anticipation of something the pleasure of which will only come to him over time through countless details. 'He cannot keep still, makes innumerable plans, begins to do things which he immediately abandons etc. For in fact this joy has been called up by an apparition of the object of his desires' (*Sketch for a Theory of the Emotions*, p. 71). His joy expresses *impatience* for the object of his desires, rather than satisfied possession of that object.

Sartre also considers a man who dances with joy because a woman has said she loves him. In dancing, the man turns his mind away from the woman herself and from the difficulties of actually possessing and sustaining her love. He takes a rest from difficulty and uncertainty and in dancing mimes his magically achieved total possession of her. 'Joy is magical behaviour which tries, by incantation, to realise the possession of the desired object as an instantaneous totality' (*Sketch for a Theory of the Emotions*, p. 72).

Joy, no less than sadness, anger, fear or any other emotion, is a magical behaviour that functions to miraculously transform a situation when that situation becomes too difficult for a person to deal with in a practical, unemotional way.

18 Contingency and Absurdity

It is not *how* things are in the world that is mystical, but *that* it exists.
(Ludwig Wittgenstein, *Tractatus Logico-Philosophicus*, prop. 6.44)

Like all philosophers, existentialists are interested in what there *is*. That is, they are interested in what there *is* in the most general or fundamental sense rather than in drawing up an infinite list of items to be found in the world. Philosophical interest in what there *is* – as opposed to what there is on the table or in the basket – is called *ontology*. Existentialists are ontologists to such an extent that the technical term for existentialism is *phenomenological ontology*.

As we saw in the early chapters of this book, what most existentialists think there *is* fundamentally is being-in-itself. Even the nothingness or non-being that existentialists talk so much about does not exist in its own right but only as a *relationship* to being-in-itself. Recall that non-being is the negation or denial of being-in-itself and as such is wholly dependent upon being-in-itself. Non-being is a being that borrows all of its being from being-in-itself. Unlike being-in-itself, it is a borrowed, derivative being.

Now, the key thing about being-in-itself that needs to be kept in mind for this chapter on contingency and absurdity is that it *is* without having to be. It absolutely *is* but nonetheless its being is not necessary. If it was necessary then its existence would be dictated by something more fundamental, dictated by necessity, whereas the thing about being-in-itself is that there is absolutely nothing more fundamental dictating and determining its existence. As a necessity it would have the characteristic of being necessary, but being-in-itself, as said, has no characteristics other than simply being.

To describe being-in-itself is always to describe it in terms of what it does not have. It is, for example, uncreated, unchanging, non-temporal and non-spatial. Creation, change, time and space are all phenomena that exist from the point of view of non-being, from the point of view of consciousness, and do not belong to being-in-itself at all.

So, the being of being-in-itself is unnecessary, superfluous, without reason to be and so on. It *is*, yet it need not be. Existentialists refer to this as the *contingency* of being-in-itself. In existentialism, as in philosophy generally, *contingent* is the opposite of *necessary*. That which is contingent is logically unnecessary or accidental, it need not be or be so. To argue that existence is contingent is to argue that it is a grotesque cosmic accident that need not exist yet happens to do so; a *de trop* existence that exists for no reason and for no purpose.

Human consciousness is capable of a sickening and terrifying awareness of being submerged in an existence that is absurd, pointless, superfluous and contingent. Sartre calls this sickening and terrifying awareness 'the Nausea' – hence the title of his famous novel. Human consciousness is, so to speak, even more contingent than the contingent existence of the universe. In having no being of its own, it exists only as a *relation* to contingency, as a mere reflection of something gratuitous. For a person to suffer the Nausea is for her to experience a ghastly state of naked, superfluous existence that not only surrounds her but is her; her mind and her body.

The contingency of existence as a whole implies that each particular thing in existence is contingent; absurd in its strange, ultimately pointless and unaccountable presence. Human activity disguises contingency by imposing meanings and purposes on the world. This is achieved largely by naming and categorising things. In naming something people believe they have made sense of it, ascribed meaning to it, grasped its essential essence, removed the contingency of its raw, nameless existence. But really, does discovering the name of a strange insect or plant, applying word labels that people have invented for these things in the past, make their existence any the less bizarre, accidental and absurd?

We tend not to think of everyday manufactured objects as absurd at all because we are so familiar with them, because we know what they are *for*. But just try looking at a table, or a mug, or a lamp, or a seat for what it is in itself, stripped of its name and function. It may take you some time and practice to 'strip it', but the claim is that if and when you do strip it, its unaccountable weirdness will freak you out. It certainly freaks out Antoine Roquentin, the central character of Sartre's novel *Nausea*. He even gets to the stage where he desperately and unsuccessfully tries to hang on to the familiar, comforting names of things. While sitting on a bus, he thinks:

> This thing on which I'm sitting, on which I leaned my hand just now, is called a seat. They made it on purpose for people to sit on ... They carried it here, into this box, and the box is now rolling and jolting along, with its rattling windows, and it's carrying this red thing inside it. I murmur: 'It's a seat,' rather like an exorcism. But the word remains on my lips, it refuses to settle on the thing. (*Nausea*, p. 180)

The truth is that things only have meaning and purpose relative to other things – words immediately link a thing to other things through language – and the whole assemblage only has the relative meaning and purpose that our ultimately pointless human activities give it. Seen for what they are in themselves, apart from the system of instrumentality that defines them or the framework of meanings that explain and justify them, objects are bewildering, peculiar, absurd, even disturbing in their contingency.

Contingency is mysterious and to be aware of contingency is to be aware of the incomprehensible existence of the universe as an utterly mysterious whole; as mystical. Ultimately, it is the very being, the very *isness* of existence that existentialists find strange, inexplicable, mysterious, absurd. Following his deeply distressing encounter with the naked existence of a tree root in the park Roquentin writes:

> I, a little while ago, experienced the absolute: the absolute or the absurd. That root – there was nothing in relation to which it was not absurd. Oh, how can I put that in words? Absurd: irreducible; nothing – not even a profound, secret aberration of Nature – could explain that. Obviously I didn't know everything, I hadn't seen the seed sprout or the tree grow. But faced with that big rugged paw, neither ignorance nor knowledge had any importance; the world of explanations and reasons is not that of existence. (*Nausea*, p. 185)

In order to make an important philosophical point, existentialists like to write novels with central characters who dwell obsessively on contingency and live always under the aspect of eternity in a meaningless, absurd universe; characters like Roquentin, or Meursault in Camus' *The Outsider*. Contrary to popular belief however, existentialists do not recommend that real life people should strive to live this way. That way lies madness.

Existentialists, unlike some of the characters they create, like most people most of the time, live and act very much in the world of relative meanings and purposes. Like most people most of the time, they keep their sanity and sense of perspective by directing their attentions to the practical task in hand, to the daily round and so on. Nonetheless, existentialists clearly hold that an occasional or background awareness of contingency and absurdity is vital if a person is to achieve any degree of authenticity and to avoid living a lie.

Existentialist philosophy is characterised by an abiding hatred and distrust of people who seem totally unaware of life's contingency and absurdity; people who, having once glimpsed life's contingency and absurdity and been terrified by it, are fleeing from it. In the existentialists' view, this flight from contingency and absurdity is a typically middle-class trait, the very core of bourgeois mentality.

The fundamental project of such people is to evade their own contingency and that of the world by acting in bad faith. The world, they tell themselves, is not contingent but *created* with humankind as its centrepiece. They assume that they have an immortal essence, that their existence is inevitable and that they exist by divine decree rather than by accident. They believe that the moral and social values to which they subscribe are objective, absolute and unquestionable.

Society as it is, as that which, in their view, is grounded in these absolute values, is seen by them to constitute the only possible reality. All they have to do to claim their absolute right to be respected by others and to have the respect of others sustain the illusion of their necessity, is to dutifully fulfil the role prescribed to them by society and identify themselves totally with that role. They learn to see themselves only as other people see them and avoid thinking about themselves in any kind of philosophical way.

Dwelling on the contingency and absurdity of existence, their own and that of the world generally, is strictly off limits for people mired in bad faith. As far as possible, they avoid thinking about anything at all, except at the most humdrum and clichéd level. They stick to small talk and the listing of mundane facts. If the conversation ever threatens to get a bit deep or philosophical they laugh nervously with embarrassment and move swiftly on. Existentialists like to view them as the most absurd thing of all, but of course, the utter contingency of the universe implies that everything is as equally absurd as everything else.

19 God

> Though she wasn't an atheist, mother had never given a thought to religion in her life. (Albert Camus, *The Outsider*, p. 12)

Existentialism and atheism have become almost synonymous terms. This is because the best known existentialist thinkers of the twentieth century, Heidegger, Sartre, de Beauvoir, Camus and Beckett, are all declared atheists who insist that mankind is abandoned in a meaningless, godless universe. Contrary to popular belief, however, atheism is not compulsory for existentialists and not all existentialists are atheists, even if most of them are. Interestingly, the philosophy of existentialism is as much rooted in the Christianity of Kierkegaard, as in the 'God is dead' atheism of Schopenhauer and Nietzsche.

Kierkegaard was only forty-two years old when he died. He dedicated his short, troubled life to the creation of a huge body of philosophical and theological writing that inspired both existentialism and modern Protestant philosophy. As all later existentialists readily acknowledge, many of the central themes and concepts of existentialism – freedom, choice, responsibility, authenticity, anxiety, despair and absurdity – originate in the writings of Kierkegaard.

Although a Christian, Kierkegaard was far from being an obedient, unquestioning sheep-like member of the Christian flock. He was very much an eccentric maverick who found himself continually at odds with orthodox Christian views generally and the Danish State Church in particular. It is Kierkegaard's radical approach to Christianity, his views on faith and religious commitment and his rejection of a rationalist approach towards the religious life, that make him a true existentialist.

In many ways Kierkegaard's philosophy is a reaction to the rationalism of the German idealist, George W. F. Hegel. Hegel argues that human reason is an historical development and that history itself is the progressive development of human reason towards perfect rationality. History is the process of Absolute Mind or God coming to know itself through the perfection of human reason. In coming to understand the nature of Absolute Mind or God perfected human reason reveals Absolute Mind or God and brings it to full reality. In other words, the mind of God as Absolute Mind becomes actual when particular human minds collectively achieve perfection.

Kierkegaard finds Hegel's idealism disturbing. He argues that in making human thought, and ultimately humankind's relationship with God, the product of an historical process, Hegel disregards the human individual. For Kierkegaard, the individual does not experience herself primarily, if at all, as a part of history, but rather as a free, anxious, despairing being troubled by concrete, existential moral concerns and existing without any purpose that reason can discover.

For Kierkegaard, Hegel's obsession with reason and rationality in his theorising about mankind's relationship to God reflects an obsession with reason and rationality that has dominated and misled Christian theology for centuries. Hegel's philosophy is the most rationally refined and therefore the most extreme expression of this obsession.

Kierkegaard is critical of traditional Christian theology for claiming that God's existence and nature can be established *objectively* and that religious and moral beliefs are, therefore, a matter of reason. For Kierkegaard, God's existence cannot be proven or even shown to be probable, as no amount of finite reasoning can establish anything at all about the infinite. Religious faith is not a matter of objective reasoning, or a matter of going along with the reasoning of others through the complacent acceptance of Church doctrine, but rather a matter of a highly personal, subjective, passionate and freely chosen commitment to believe.

Kierkegaard's philosophy has inspired, and continues to inspire, generations of religious existentialists, among them Karl Jaspers, Paul Tillich, Martin Buber, Karl Barth and Gabriel Marcel. According to de Beauvoir, it was Marcel who first coined the word 'existentialist' (*The Prime of Life*, p. 548). Echoing Kierkegaard, these philosophers and theologians criticise the dominant role that reason has come to play in religion, stressing instead the importance of a highly personal and passionate commitment to live according to a set of religious values that cannot be rationally justified.

For religious existentialists, genuine religious faith is not about passively adopting certain communal beliefs by assenting to questionable propositions, it is about one's moment by moment attitude to life, death and the infinite. Faith is not an established viewpoint but an ongoing act of will maintained in the face of doubts, misgivings, challenges and difficulties. A person never simply *has* faith, her faith is something she must continually create. The person who believes she possess faith, as one can posses a car, is inauthentic; her faith is not genuine.

Religious existentialism adheres to the general existentialist maxim that to be is to do, and certainly for religious existentialists the true measure of faith is action. Kierkegaard wrote a highly influential book, *Fear and Trembling*, under the pseudonym of Johannes de Silentio, in which he explores the faith of Abraham.

In the Bible (Genesis 22:1–19), God tells Abraham to travel to the land of Moriah and sacrifice his only son Isaac. The biblical account does not explore Abraham's thoughts but we can imagine, as Kierkegaard does, that Abraham is horrified by God's command. Nonetheless, by his actions, Abraham places his faith in God higher than anything else of value in his life and does as God orders. At the last moment, when Abraham has demonstrated the power of his faith, the power of his will, God allows him to sacrifice a ram instead of Isaac.

Religious existentialists argue that authentic religious faith must be like the faith of Abraham – a man who has come to be known as The Father of Faith. It must be suffered, realised through action, highly subjective and personal and sustained by a freely chosen will to believe that may well go against reason, the advice of other people and even ordinary moral considerations. Religious existentialists urge each individual to have the kind of authentic relationship with God exemplified by Abraham rather than just 'go through the motions' of so-called belief in an anonymous, conformist, passive, dispassionate, sheep-like way. For Kierkegaard, to exist, and therefore to have a relationship with the infinite, is comparable to riding a wild stallion. Unfortunately, most people 'exist' as though they had fallen asleep in a hay wagon.

For the atheistic existentialists, all faith is bad faith. In their view, the position of the religious existentialists regarding religious faith and the existence of God indicates a primitive project of bad faith in which people choose to believe what suits them. The kind of bad faith that, as Sartre argues, 'stands forth in the firm resolution *not to demand too much*, to count itself satisfied when it is barely persuaded, to force itself in decisions to adhere to uncertain truths' (*Being and Nothingness*, p. 91).

The atheistic existentialists certainly question the spiritual direction of the philosophy of the religious existentialists, but not their view that every person is an indeterminate and necessarily free being anxiously striving to fulfil herself and to give her absurd existence meaning. All existentialists share Kierkegaard's view of the self as indeterminate and ambiguous, his view that a person is nothing other than what she chooses to be.

A person is free and cannot cease to be free. She cannot become a fixed, determinate being so as to be rid of herself as a being that must *strive* in vain to be fixed and determinate. Kierkegaard notes throughout *The Sickness unto Death* that the self despairs, unto death, of achieving oneness with itself, just as it despairs of being rid of itself as a self that despairs of achieving oneness with itself. Kierkegaard's notion of the self, despairing both of being itself and of escaping itself, continues to have a huge influence on both theistic and atheistic existentialism.

The atheistic existentialists look to Nietzsche for inspiration as much as to Kierkegaard. Nietzsche followed Schopenhauer in arguing that for intelligent people the idea of God is obsolete as an explanation of the way things are. A position he summed up in his famous maxim, 'God is dead'. The atheistic existentialists certainly see the idea of God as obsolete as an explanation of the way things are. In their view, to believe in God is to refuse to confront reality for what it is, to believe in a fairy tale as a means of obscuring the hard existential truths of human reality. Sartre, approaching old age, wrote these chilling words:

> My retrospective illusions are in pieces. Martyrdom, salvation, immortality: all are crumbling, the building is falling in ruins. I have caught the Holy Ghost in the cellars and flung him out of them. Atheism is a cruel, long-term business: I believe I have gone through it to the end. (*Words*, p. 157)

The atheistic existentialists do not actually go to great lengths to prove God does not exist. The indifference of nature to human suffering and the horrors and injustices that occur every day in the world are for them strong evidence for the non-existence of an all-powerful, benevolent God. They tend to see the burden of proof as lying with those who believe in such a peculiar entity as a moral Supreme Being who created the universe, and they take as read the standard *objections* to the ontological, cosmological and teleological arguments for God's existence.

Most if not all arguments for God's existence can be classified as a version of one or other of these three *theistic* arguments. Very basically, ontological arguments assert that the idea of God implies the existence of God, cosmological arguments assert that God is the uncaused cause of everything and teleological arguments assert that the universe shows evidence of intelligent design.

The standard objections to the theistic arguments, objections made by philosophers such as Hume and Kant, are well documented elsewhere, so I won't explore them in any detail, suffice to say that logically the idea of a thing cannot imply the existence of that thing, the notion of an uncaused cause is nonsensical and there are scientific theories, primarily the theory of evolution, that explain nature without appealing to the notion of intelligent design. For detailed consideration of the theistic arguments and the various refutations of them see *Philosophy of Religion* by John H. Hick.

As well as endorsing the standard objections to the theistic arguments, the atheistic existentialists offer various arguments of their own against God's existence. One of their main arguments is that God cannot exist as He is supposed to exist – as an omnipresent, transcendent, disembodied consciousness – because every consciousness must be *embodied*.

To be conscious is to be conscious of a world from a particular point of view, the point of view of the physical body. As we have seen, consciousness is not something that happens to be attached to the body, as though it could exist independently of the body. Consciousness is *necessarily* embodied in that it exists only as the transcendence of the facticity of its immediate bodily situation and not as a transcendent being in its own right. The body is always the immediate and inescapable situation of any consciousness. For the atheistic existentialists, this argument also demolishes the claim that there is an afterlife beyond the death of the physical body.

Another argument that the atheistic existentialists put forward is the argument against the possibility of *being-for-itself-in-itself*. This argument was explored in Chapter 3 on nothingness but it is worth considering again specifically as an argument for the impossibility of a divine consciousness.

Essentially, theists conceive God to be a being-for-itself; a conscious, knowing being. God's consciousness, however, is held to exist fundamentally rather than as a relation or a negation in the manner of ordinary consciousness. That is, God's existence and essence are held to be one, or, in existentialist terms, God's being-for-itself is held to exist in itself. In short, God is held to be the ultimate being-for-itself-in-itself. The above mentioned ontological argument for the existence of God assumes this unity of existence and essence. For the medieval philosopher, St Anselm, for example, the most perfect conceivable entity must have the attribute of existence. So, for Anselm, God's essence *implies* his existence.

As said, every being-for-itself, every consciousness, desires to be God because every being-for-itself strives to be a being-for-itself-in-itself that has completely fulfilled itself and achieved identity with itself. In other words, every being-for-itself strives to be a non-being that *is* its own non-being so as to escape being a non-being that *has to be* its own non-being as the negation of being-in-itself. Crucially, the desired unity of being-for-itself and being-in-itself is impossible to achieve because being-for-itself must always be the negation or denial of being-in-itself. Negation or non-being can never coincide with or achieve unity with the being it negates. The logical and ontological impossibility of this unity is the impossibility of the existence of God.

The atheistic existentialists also argue against creationism. If the being of the universe was conceived and created in the divine mind or subjectivity of God *ex nihilo* (out of nothing) it remains only a mode of God's subjectivity. It cannot even have a semblance of objectivity. It cannot exist in its own right as a genuine creation that is independent of God.

Moreover, if the being of the universe is *perpetually* created by God, as some creationist theories suppose, then the being of the universe would have no substantiality of its own, its being would be perpetually derived from the being of God. Once more, it would remain a mode of God's subjectivity lacking any real objectivity.

The atheistic existentialists conclude that even if being was created it is inexplicable as a creation. Being must be absolutely independent of God in order to be that which is, and must be, its own foundation. Such absolute independence means not only that God, if He exists, does not intervene in the universe, but that He absolutely cannot intervene. Interestingly, this view is akin to the theological standpoint of *deism*.

For the atheistic existentialists, to look honestly at the world and at human existence is to see that, as they say, *existence precedes essence*. To suppose that there is a God is to suppose the opposite, to suppose that *essence precedes existence*. It is to assert that human beings are conceived in the mind of God and therefore have a nature that is fixed for all time. Such idealism is fundamentally opposed to the central view of atheistic existentialism that human beings are essentially free and self-defining. As Nietzsche says, '… what would there be to create if gods – existed!' (*Thus Spoke Zarathustra*, p. 111). For his part, Sartre says:

> Atheistic existentialism, of which I am a representative, declares … that if God does not exist there is at least one being whose existence comes before its essence, a being which exists before it can be defined by any conception of it. That being is man or, as Heidegger has it, the human reality. What do we mean by saying that existence precedes essence? We mean that man first of all exists, encounters himself, surges up in the world – and defines himself afterwards. (*Existentialism and Humanism*, pp. 27–28)

According to Schopenhauer, the death of God, the loss of the idea of God as a credible explanation of the universe and humankind's place in it, plunges people into nihilism and despair. Life, the universe and everything can have no meaning, purpose or value if there is no God to give it meaning, purpose or value. It is often thought that because of its rejection of God, atheistic existentialism is utterly nihilistic and despairing in the Schopenhauerian sense. This, however, is not the case. Atheistic existentialism takes its cue from Nietzsche's *anti-nihilism* rather than Schopenhauer's nihilism and is, despite its interest in anxiety, absurdity and death, an ultimately upbeat and optimistic philosophy.

Reacting to Schopenhauer, who influenced him greatly, Nietzsche attempts to push Schopenhauer's nihilism to its ultimate conclusion, to demolish faith in religious based values to such an extent that the way is made clear for a 're-evaluation of all values' including moral values.

For Nietzsche, nihilism carried to its conclusion annihilates itself as a value and becomes anti-nihilism. To overcome nihilism people must overcome the guilt and despair of having killed God, having killed the *idea* of God. To achieve this, people must aspire to become gods themselves by becoming the source of their own values and by always taking responsibility for who they are and what they do.

The atheistic existentialists strongly endorse Nietzsche's rejection of metaphysics and idealism; his rejection of the illusion of worlds-behind-the-scene. They agree with Nietzsche that reality does not lurk behind appearances in some other-worldly realm. What appears *is* reality. As there is nothing beyond appearances, the primary task of philosophy is to honestly describe the world and human existence as they are without resorting to speculative metaphysical and religious explanations that aim primarily at providing false comfort. 'The existentialist', Sartre insists, 'finds it extremely embarrassing that God does not exist, for there disappears with Him all possibility of finding values in an intelligible heaven' (*Existentialism and Humanism*, p. 33).

Nietzsche, Heidegger, Sartre, de Beauvoir, Camus and the rest of the atheistic existentialists are not the kind of atheists who simply dismiss God's existence and think no more about it, but atheists who are moved by the profound implications of God's non-existence for human reality and morality. They recognise that the non-existence of God implies that all existence, including human existence, is without *ultimate* meaning, purpose or value. But they do not rest there.

In a move that fundamentally defines their brand of existentialism, they strive to forge an ultimately anti-nihilistic philosophy from a starkly nihilistic initial position. They each argue in their own way that to reach their full potential people must overcome the inauthenticity and cowardice involved in clinging to the age old comfort-blanket of improbable religious beliefs. People must stop mistakenly assuming that a moralising celestial authority has preordained the nature and scope of their existence, and instead recognise that life has only the meaning, purpose and value that each individual person chooses to give it.

20   Death

It hath been often said, that it is not death but dying which is terrible.
(Henry Fielding, *Amelia*, p. 103)

There are a million ways to die, but existentially speaking, death has only
two faces. There is the death we experience, the death of the Other, so
emotionally painful and bewildering when it is the death of a *significant*
other, and there is the death we do not experience, our own death, the
fear of which nonetheless haunts many a person's thoughts.

Certainly, some people are haunted almost constantly by their fear
of death, and a few are even prepared to talk about it. Samuel Johnson
admitted to having a terrible fear of his own death, his own dying,
while Thomas de Quincey, in *Confessions of an English Opium-Eater*,
tells how even the brightest, liveliest summer days induced in him the
thought of death. 'The exuberant and riotous prodigality of life naturally forces the mind more powerfully upon the antagonist thought of
death, and the wintry sterility of the grave' (*Confessions of an English
Opium-Eater*, p. 83). Philip Roth's novel, *Everyman,* is a disturbingly
matter of fact account of an ageing man confronting his irretrievably
failing health and the brute truth that he has only oblivion to look
forward to. Leo Tolstoy's preoccupation with death and the meaning of
mortality is reflected in his great novel, *Anna Karenina*, particularly in
the thoughts and fears of Levin, a character closely based on Tolstoy
himself.

Levin is present at the deathbed of his brother Nikolái. Tolstoy describes Nikolái's slow, agonising death in chilling, existential detail. It is one of the most moving and disturbing scenes in literature, yet it is simply a brutally honest account of an ordinary, everyday deathbed struggle.

> Suffering, steadily increasing, did its part in preparing him for death. There was no position in which he did not suffer, no moment when he was oblivious, no part or limb of his body that did not hurt, that did not torment him. Even this body's memories, impressions and thoughts now evoked in him the same revulsion as the body itself. The sight of other people, their conversation, his own memories – all this was sheer torment to him. Those around him felt it and unconsciously forbade themselves any free movement, conversation, expression of their wishes. His whole life merged into one feeling of suffering and the wish to be rid of it. (*Anna Karenina*, p. 503)

Tolstoy's harrowing account of Nikolái's dying is particularly terrifying to any reader who sees in it a possible account of her own dying. It is hard to imagine how any reader could avoid thinking: 'If I do not die quickly in an accident, this is more or less how my own final days and hours will be. I'll reach a level of physical and mental suffering way beyond any illness or hangover I've ever experienced. Only children in their naivety and youthful confusion fear being dead. What I fear is this terrible business of dying. That I must be tasked so harshly to obtain oblivion just when I feel so ill.' Yet there are many people, it seems, who would see in Tolstoy's account of Nikolái's dying only Nikolái's dying and not their own dying at all.

Amazingly perhaps, some people claim never to think seriously about their own mortality. What are we philosophers and existentialists and generally gloomy souls to make of them? Are they lying, are they incredibly obtuse? If they really never seriously think about their dying then they are certainly lucky, exempt from the average thinking person's burden of morbidity. Perhaps they are wise. They have quickly learnt to be too busy living to dwell even for a second on their mortality. After all, there is nothing they can do about their mortality other than seek uncertain ways to postpone the inevitable. So why talk about it, think about it, worry about it? Why not indulge in some healthy bad faith and always instantly dismiss the subject as ridiculous and improper whenever it threatens to rear its ugly head?

Nietzsche, a deep thinker who undoubtedly did more than his fair share of pondering death and dying, marvels at how most people are disinclined to think about death. How instead they throw themselves into living as though they were immortal, as though all their little plans and schemes meant something in the grand scheme of things. He sees this thirst for life as a kind of drunkenness, a madness. But it is a healthy madness, a beneficial foolishness that he admires and is pleased to observe, even if he is unable to fully indulge in it himself. As he writes in *The Gay Science*:

> *The thought of death.* – Living in the midst of this jumble of little lanes, needs and voices gives me a melancholy happiness: how much enjoyment, impatience, and desire, how much thirsty life and drunkenness of life comes to light every moment! And yet silence will soon descend on all these noisy, living, life-thirsty people. How his shadow stands even now behind everyone, as his dark fellow traveller! It is always like the last moment before the departure of an emigrants' ship: people have more to say to each other than ever, the hour is late, and the ocean and its desolate silence are waiting impatiently behind all of this noise – so covetous and certain of their prey. And all and every one of them suppose that the past was little or nothing while the near future is everything; and that is the reason for all of this haste, this clamour, this shouting out and overreaching each other. Everyone wants to be the first in this future – and yet death and deathly silence alone are certain and common to all in this future. How strange it is that this sole certainty and common element makes almost no impression on people, and that nothing is further from their minds than the feeling that they form a brotherhood of death. It makes me happy that men do not want at all to think the thought of death! (*The Gay Science,* 278, pp. 224–225)

Even morbid philosophers and novelists busily embrace life more or less as Nietzsche describes, writing about death in as lively a way as possible, as though they believed that by their writing they were making some scrap of difference to their ultimate destiny. How else could they live, how else could anyone live? The stark reality of death cannot change the fact that, as the old saying goes, life is for the living.

The general position of the existentialists with regard to death, with regard to life for that matter, is that to be *authentic* a person should be clearly aware of the hard, inescapable, existential truth of her mortality; aware that her life is a *finite project*. This awareness should spur her relentlessly towards positive, decisive, courageous action rather than sink her into a paralysing fear of death that amounts to a fear of life and a failure to live it to the full.

My exploration of authenticity in Chapter 10 ended with a promise to return in this final chapter to Heidegger's notion of *authentic-being-towards-death*. Like the other existentialists, Heidegger holds that the project of authenticity involves a person affirming the inescapable, existential truths of the human condition. However, whereas the accounts of authenticity offered by Sartre, de Beauvoir, Camus and others emphasise the affirmation of freedom, Heidegger's account of authenticity, as put forward in his major work, *Being and Time*, emphasises the affirmation of mortality. Authenticity for Heidegger is primarily authentic being-towards-death.

As previously explained, Heidegger refers to a person's presence in the world as *Dasein*. *Dasein* literally mean *being-there* and refers to a person's unique spatial and temporal situatedness in the world. Heidegger insists that 'Death is Dasein's *ownmost* possibility' (*Being and Time*, p. 307). For Heidegger, the constant possibility of death in the present, the inevitability of death in the future, is central to the very being of Dasein.

A person's present is what it is by virtue of its finitude, a finitude arising directly from the promise of death that perpetually haunts the present. Authentic being-towards-death involves a person fully acknowledging her finitude and the inevitability of her death in the way she lives her life. By recognising that she herself must die, rather than merely considering death to be something that happens to other people, something that happened, for example, to an unfortunate character in a Tolstoy novel, a person ceases to view herself as simply another Other and realises that she exists as the wholly unique possibility of her own death. Heidegger says, 'The non-relational character of death, as understood in anticipation, individualises Dasein down to itself' (*Being and Time*, p. 308).

Only by realising that she is the utterly unique possibility of her own death does she cease to treat herself as though she is a copy of the next person and of all people. For Heidegger, this is the real meaning of authenticity. The authentic person, like the authentic work of art, is the genuine article, not a reproduction or a replica. Though her life may *resemble* the lives of many others, she is, nonetheless, unique, and what makes her unique above all else is that only she can and will die her death.

A bodyguard throws himself in the line of fire and takes the fatal bullet meant for the president. The bodyguard has 'died for the president' but he has not thereby died the president's death. Only the president can die the president's death at some point in the future. '*No one can take the Other's dying away from him* ... Dying is something that every Dasein itself must take upon itself at the time. By its very essence, death is in every case mine, in so far as it "is" at all' (*Being and Time*, p. 284).

In Heidegger's view, it is only when a person fully realises that she must die and acts in accordance with this realisation that she truly begins to exist and live in her own right. In taking responsibility for her own death she takes responsibility for her own life and the way in which she chooses to live it. For Heidegger, to truly realise and affirm mortality is to overcome bad faith. This view concurs with the claim made directly or indirectly by all existentialists that authenticity involves living without regret.

If the positive affirmation of freedom demands that a person affirm her entire life without regret, then it follows that she must also affirm her mortality. This does not mean she must take pleasure in the prospect of death – 'The thought of suicide is a powerful solace: by means of it one gets through many a bad night' (Nietzsche, *Beyond Good and Evil*, 157, p. 103) – but it does mean she must acknowledge that her life is finite and the implications of this for the way she lives her life.

Nietzsche formed the idea of the ideal *Ubermensch* (overman). An overman creates himself, he is the source of his own values. He has achieved authenticity and true greatness of spirit by overcoming himself and all his regrets. A key characteristic of Nietzsche's overman is his recognition and acceptance of his own mortality. The overman is a person who, though fully aware of his mortality, is not petrified with fear at the thought of it. He does not allow his fear of death to prevent him from taking certain risks and living his life to the full.

Simone de Beauvoir, who took many risks in her life, particularly during the German occupation of France, argues that this attitude towards death is an essential characteristic of the adventurous person who values the affirmation of his or her freedom above timid self-preservation. 'Even his death is not an evil since he is a man only in so far as he is mortal: he must assume it as the natural limit of his life, as the risk implied by every step' (*The Ethics of Ambiguity*, p. 82).

Although Heidegger's thoughts on affirming mortality concur with de Beauvoir and Sartre's thoughts on affirming freedom, the fact remains that Sartre objects to the concept of being-towards-death that lies at the heart of Heidegger's theory of authenticity. This is worth exploring as it reveals further insights into the phenomenon of death.

Sartre certainly agrees with Heidegger that embracing life's finitude is a prompt to authentic action. He agrees with Heidegger that a person who embraces her finitude is motivated to commit courageously to a course of action rather than hold back in cowardly and ultimately futile self-preservation. He agrees also that embracing finitude inspires a person to reject mediocrity, what Heidegger calls *everydayness*, in favour of being all that she can be. Sartre, however, disagrees with Heidegger that death is a person's *ownmost* possibility – the possibility that is most her own. Indeed, Sartre argues that death is not one of a person's possibilities at all. As the absolute limit of all of a person's possibilities it is not itself a possibility.

Sartre insists that a person does not die her own death because her own death is not an event she can experience. From her own point of view, she does not undergo death. How could she, when death is the utter annihilation of the point of view that she is? In a very real sense, death only happens to other people. Only the death of other people is an event in my life, just as my death can only be an event in the lives of those who outlive me. Reflecting on a serious cycling accident that nearly killed her, Simone de Beauvoir writes:

> I had had a close brush with death. Considering the terror which death had always aroused in me, to have come so very near to it was, for me, a highly significant event. 'I might never have wakened again,' I told myself, and suddenly the business of dying seemed out of all proportion … in the most literal and precise sense, death is *nothing*. A *person* never is dead; there is no longer a 'person' to sustain the concept of 'death'. I felt I had finally exorcised my fears on this score. (*The Prime of Life*, p. 497)

Sartre and de Beauvoir are surely quite right that one's own death is not an event in one's own life and that it is therefore irrational to fear death. However, as has already been suggested, it is not actually death that most people fear but the physical and mental agony of dying. Admittedly, even a terminally ill person does not know for sure at any moment that she is just about to die because she may yet make a temporary recovery. But surely, she must know when she has entered into the final stages of her terminal illness. There must come a point when she accepts that there is no longer any hope of a genuine recovery, of a return to relative health or reasonable quality of life, that it is, as we say, only a matter of time.

Tolstoy's Nikolái hoped to make a recovery from what was generally understood to be a terminal illness even when that illness was far advanced. But at the stage of *extremity* described in the passage above, even *he* knew that the game was up, that he was now dying, that there was no way back, that give or take a day or two he would be dead. De Beauvoir, then, is surely saying two things: she had exorcised her fear of *death* because death is nothing, and she had exorcised her fear of the kind of *dying* that follows an instantaneous and unexpected loss of consciousness. Surely, she cannot be saying that she had exorcised her fear of dying in the manner of poor Nikolái: slowly, painfully and fully conscious.

In Sartre's view, a person who is genuinely aware of her mortality and lives her life accordingly is not thereby subject to a sense of being-towards-death like a condemned prisoner awaiting execution. Sartre even argues that a person who views her death as being nearer today than it was yesterday is mistaken. She will, of course, live for a certain number of days, but she is mistaken if she thinks that with each day that passes she is using up a sort of quota. She is mistaken because she does not have a quota. She could die now or tomorrow or years from now. It is inevitable that she will die eventually, but the time of her death is not predetermined.

This seems a fair argument so long as we are not talking about a person *in extremis*. Surely, Nikolái knows, in the sense described above, that his death will come very soon. But of course, as Sartre would insist, he cannot sense death approaching like a storm and does not know the *precise* moment when he will expire.

Sartre's main point is that when a person is dead, others will give the total of her years, but this total was not fixed in advance while she was alive and her life was not a process of fulfilling it. Only a condemned person has a quota of days, but even a condemned person can be reprieved unexpectedly or killed by flu before reaching the guillotine. The point is that the closeness of death changes with circumstances. If a person was in a high fever yesterday, she was closer to death yesterday than she is today now that she has recovered.

So, a person does not experience her mortality, her finitude, as such. A person does not experience herself as progressing towards an encounter with the nothingness and annihilation of death; as a being-towards-death. Even a person *in extremis*, though she knows the end is near, does not know the exact distance to the finishing line or exactly when she will get there. And in getting there, *she* will not get there, for *she* will have ceased to be.

Simone de Beauvoir died in 1986 but her mortal soul and her mortal fears live on in the following passage, set down by way of conclusion to this chapter and this existentialist's guide to death, the universe and nothingness:

> It sometimes seemed to me that if I succeeded in being *there* at the exact instant of my death, if I coincided with it, then I would compel it to *be*: this would be one way of preserving it. But no, I thought, death will never lie within my grasp; never will I be able to concentrate all the horror with which it fills me into one final, all-embracing spasm of anguish. There is no help for it, the small squeamish fear will remain, the persistent night thoughts, the banal image of a black ruled line terminating the series of measured spaces that stand for years – and after it nothing but a blank page. I shall never apprehend death; all I will ever know is this illusive foretaste, mingled with the flavour of my living days. (*The Prime of Life*, p. 604)

Bibliography

Adams, Douglas, *The Hitchhiker's Guide to the Galaxy: A Trilogy in Four Parts* (London: Pan, 1992).

Adler, Alfred, *The Neurotic Constitution: Outlines of a Comparative Individualistic Psychology and Psychotherapy* (London and New York: Routledge, 1999).

Brentano, Franz, *Psychology from an Empirical Standpoint*, trans. A. Rancurello, D. Terrell and L. McAlister (London and New York: Routledge, 2004).

Camus, Albert, *The Myth of Sisyphus*, trans. Justin O'Brien (London: Penguin, 2006).

____ *The Outsider* (*The Stranger*), trans. Joseph Laredo (London: Penguin, 2003).

Carroll, Lewis, *Through the Looking Glass* (London: Penguin, 2007).

Castaneda, Carlos, *The Second Ring of Power* (London: Penguin Arkana, 1990).

de Beauvoir, Simone, *The Ethics of Ambiguity*, trans. Bernard Frechtman (New York: Citadel Press, 2000).

____ *The Prime of Life*, trans. Peter Green (London: Penguin, 2001).

____ *The Second Sex*, trans. Constance Borde and Sheila Malovany-Chevallier (London: Jonathan Cape, 2009).

____ *She Came to Stay*, trans. Yvonne Moyse and Roger Senhouse (London and New York: Harper Perennial, 2006).

Defoe, Daniel, *Robinson Crusoe* (London: Penguin, 2004).

De Quincey, Thomas, *Confessions of an English Opium-Eater* (London: Penguin, 2003).

Dostoevsky, Fyodor, *Crime and Punishment*, trans. David Magarshack (London: Penguin, 2007).

Fielding, Henry, *Amelia* (London: Penguin, 1987).

Greene, Graham, *The Power and the Glory* (London: Vintage, 2004).

Grene, Marjorie, *Sartre* (Lanham, MD: University Press of America, 1983).

Hegel, George Wilhelm Friedrich, *The Phenomenology of Mind*, trans. J. B. Bailey (New York: Dover, 2003).

Heidegger, Martin, *Being and Time,* trans. John Macquarrie and Edward Robinson (Oxford: Blackwell, 1993).

Hick, John H., *Philosophy of Religion* (Englewood Cliffs, NJ: Prentice-Hall, 1990).

Kant, Immanuel, *Critique of Pure Reason*, trans. Norman Kemp Smith (London: Macmillan, 2003).

Kierkegaard, Søren, *The Concept of Anxiety, Kierkegaard's Writings Vol. 8* (Princeton, NJ: Princeton University Press, 1981).

_____ *Fear and Trembling*, trans. Alastair Hannay (London: Penguin, 1985).

_____ *The Sickness unto Death*, trans. Alastair Hannay (London: Penguin, 1989).

Laing, Ronald D., *The Divided Self: An Existential Study in Sanity and Madness* (London: Penguin, 1990).

Merleau-Ponty, Maurice, *Phenomenology of Perception*, trans. Colin Smith (London and New York: Routledge, 2002).

Midgley, Mary, *Beast and Man: The Roots of Human Nature* (London and New York: Routledge, 2002).

Nietzsche, Friedrich, *Beyond Good and Evil: Prelude to a Philosophy of the Future*, trans. R. J. Hollingdale (London: Penguin, 2003).

_____ *Ecce Homo: How one Becomes What One Is*, trans. R. J. Hollingdale (London: Penguin, 2004).

_____ *The Gay Science*, trans. Walter Kaufmann (New York: Vintage Press, 1974).

_____ *Human, All-too-Human: A Book for Free Spirits*, trans. R. J. Hollingdale (Cambridge: Cambridge University Press, 1996).

_____ *Thus Spoke Zarathustra*, trans. R. J. Hollingdale (London: Penguin, 1988).

Roosevelt, Eleanor, *You Learn by Living: Eleven Keys for a More Fulfilling Life* (London: Harper Perennial, 2011).

Roth, Philip, *Everyman* (London: Jonathan Cape, 2006).

Sartre, Jean-Paul ,*The Age of Reason*, trans. David Caute (London: Penguin, 2001).

____ *Being and Nothingness: An Essay on Phenomenological Ontology,* trans. Hazel E. Barnes (London and New York: Routledge, 2003).

____ *Existentialism and Humanism*, trans. Philip Mairet (London: Methuen, 1993).

____ *The Family Idiot* Vols. 1–5, trans. Carol Cosman (Chicago, IL: University of Chicago Press, 1981).

____ *In Camera (Behind Closed Doors* or *No Exit)*, trans. Stuart Gilbert, in *In Camera and Other Plays* (London: Penguin, 1990).

____ *Nausea*, trans. Robert Baldick (London: Penguin, 2000).

____ *Sketch for a Theory of the Emotions*, trans. Philip Mairet (London: Methuen, 1985).

____ *The Transcendence of the Ego, A Sketch for a Phenomenological Description*, trans. Andrew Brown (London and New York: Routledge, 2004).

____ *Truth and Existence,* trans. Adrian van den Hoven (Chicago, IL: University of Chicago Press, 1995).

____ *War Diaries: Notebooks from a Phoney War, 1939–1940*, trans. Quintin Hoare (London: Verso, 2000).

____ *Words*, trans. Irene Clephane (London: Penguin, 2000).

Shaw, George Bernard, *Man and Superman and Three Other Plays* (New York: Barnes & Noble, 2004)

Tolstoy, Leo, *Anna Karenina*, trans. Richard Pevear and Larissa Volokhonsky (London: Penguin, 2006).

Valéry, Paul, *Mauvaises Pensées et Autres (Bad Thoughts and Others)* (Paris: Gallimard, 1942).

Wittgenstein, Ludwig, *Tractatus Logico-Philosophicus*, trans. D. F. Pears and B. F. McGuiness (London and New York: Routledge, 2001).

Woolf, Virginia, *Monday or Tuesday* (Whitefish, MT: Kessinger, 2004).

Wordsworth, William, '*The Affliction of Margaret*', in *The Collected Poems of William Wordsworth* (Ware: Wordsworth Editions, 1994).

Other Media References

Allen, Woody, *Love and Death* (United Artists, 1975).

— *Play It Again, Sam* (Paramount Pictures, 1972).

Apocalypse Now (United Artists, 1979).

The Doors, 'Riders on the Storm', Track 10, *L.A. Woman* (Elektra, 1971).

Sister Sledge, 'Lost in Music', Track 2, *We Are Family* (Cotillion, 1979).

Der Spiegel (*The Mirror*), 17 Oct 1988.

Wham!, 'Young Guns (Go for It!)', Track 8, *Fantastic* (Innervision, 1983).

Further Reading

Blackham, Harold John, *Six Existentialist Thinkers* (London and New York: Routledge, 1991).

Cox, Gary, *How to be an Existentialist, or How to Get Real, Get a Grip and Stop Making Excuses* (London and New York: Continuum, 2009).

— *The Sartre Dictionary* (London and New York: Continuum, 2008).

— *Sartre and Fiction* (London and New York: Continuum, 2009).

— *Sartre: A Guide for the Perplexed* (London and New York: Continuum, 2006).

Earnshaw, Stephen, *Existentialism: A Guide for the Perplexed* (London and New York: Continuum, 2006).

Fullbrook, Edward and Fullbrook, Kate, *Simone de Beauvoir: A Critical Introduction* (Cambridge: Polity, 1997).

Hammond, Michael, Howarth, Jane and Keat, Russell, *Understanding Phenomenology* (Oxford: Blackwell, 1992).

Heidegger, Martin, *Basic Writings*, ed. David Farrell Krell (London and New York: Routledge, 2010).

Loy, David, *Lack and Transcendence: The Problem of Death and Life in Psychotherapy, Existentialism and Buddhism* (New York: Prometheus, 2003).

Marino, Gordon D., *Basic Writings of Existentialism* (New York: Random House, 2004).

Nehamas, Alexander, *Nietzsche: Life as Literature* (Cambridge, MA: Harvard University Press, 1985).

Panza, Christopher and Gale, Gregory, *Existentialism for Dummies* (Oxford: Wiley-Blackwell, 2008).

Storr, Anthony, *Freud: A Very Short Introduction* (Oxford: Oxford University Press, 2001).

van Deurzen, Emmy and Smith, Martin, *Skills in Existential Counselling and Psychotherapy* (London: Sage, 2011).

Warnock, Mary, *Existentialism* (Oxford: Oxford University Press, 1992).

West, David, *Continental Philosophy* (Cambridge: Polity Press, 2010).

Index